I0559642

EMERGING TECHNOLOGIES IN MEDIA AND ENTERTAINMENT

MATTHEW N. O. SADIKU, Ph.D., P.E.

REGENTS PROFESSOR EMERITUS AND IEEE LIFE FELLOW
PRAIRIE VIEW A&M UNIVERSITY
PRAIRIE VIEW, TX 77446
EMAIL: SADIKU@IEEE.ORG
WEB: WWW.MATTHEW-SADIKU.COM

BOOK FILMS MEDIA

Copyright © 2025 Matthew N. O. Sadiku

All rights reserved. *No part of this publication may be reproduced, distributed, or transmitted in any form or by any means, including photocopying, recording, or other electronic or mechanical methods, without the prior written permission of the publisher, except as permitted by U.S. copyright law. For permission requests, contact:*

support@bookfilmsmedia.com

Date published: September, 01 2025

Matthew N. O. Sadiku
sadiku@ieee.org
www.matthew-sadiku.com

Paperback: 978-1-967753-28-4
eBook: 978-1-967753-29-1
Hardcover: 978-1-967753-30-7

BookFilmsMedia
2780 South Jones Blvd Suite 200 - 4007
Las Vegas, NV 89146 United States
+1 725 - 238 - 6534

Cover Image: R. Williamson, "Media and entertainment: How this industry is impacted by big data," January 2021,
https://www.datasciencecentral.com/media-and-entertainment-how-this-industry-is-impacted-by-big-data/

DEDICATED TO MY WIFE:

JANET O. SADIKU

BRIEF TABLE OF CONTENTS

PREFACE

Earlier, people used to spend their quality time with their friends and family sitting around the campfire. Today, with rapid advancement in technology, the television had become a main base of entertainment. Today, the term "media" encompasses not only television, radio and print, but also phone calls, text messaging, social platforms, and video chatting — any channel through which information and entertainment is disseminated. The entertainment sector is a huge umbrella term involving a large number of sub-industries devoted to entertainment. The media and entertainment (M&E) industries can be partitioned into four main verticals: film, music, book publishing and video games. They have frequently been at the forefront of adopting new technologies. Since the dawn of broadcasting, technology advancements have enabled the industry to continually create ever-more entertaining and informative experiences for audiences everywhere.

The media and entertainment industry is driven by technology. In this technological evolving world, we must adopt the latest technologies to boost success. The media and entertainment industry is undergoing a significant transformation, driven by emerging technologies that are redefining how content is created, delivered, and consumed. By harnessing emerging technologies, media companies can deliver tailored content and craft interactive environments that cater to individual preferences.

This book explores emerging technologies used in the media and entertainment (M&E) industry. It is organized into 10 chapters that summarize emerging M&E technologies: artificial intelligence, artificial intelligence, robotics, drones, cloud computing, big data, blockchain, Internet of things, immersive technologies, 5G network, and biometrics.

Chapter 1 - Introduction

This chapter looks at the top emerging technologies in the media and entertainment industry. It serves as introduction to the entire book. Technology plays an incredible role in the media and entertainment. Emerging technologies are shaping our societies. This chapter provides a brief introduction to emerging technologies in the media and entertainment industry. Such technologies include artificial intelligence, robotics, drones, cloud computing, big data, blockchain, Internet of things, immersive technologies, 5G network, and biometrics.

Chapter 2 - Artificial Intelligence

In this chapter, we explore some popular use cases of artificial intelligence (AI) in the media and entertainment industry. The key benefit of integrating artificial intelligence into the entertainment and media industry is its ability to efficiently analyze large amounts of data. From automating creative processes to enhancing audience engagement, AI is revolutionizing entertainment by transforming how content is created, personalized, and experienced. AI in entertainment holds immense potential to impact the industry and provide audiences with unprecedented engagement and enjoyment.

Chapter 3 - Robotics

This chapter examines the role of robots in media and entertainment. The robots are shaped and designed to look like humans and can also be programmed to perform complex tasks and movements. Robotic technologies are applied in many areas of media and entertainment. They are hoisting pop stars over our heads, dancing with pianos, making cameos in blockbuster movies, and creating spectacles of color and light in venues large and small. The entertainment industry is witnessing a revolutionary convergence of technology and creativity through the incorporation of robots.

Chapter 4 - Drones

In this chapter, we explore the role of drones in the media and entertainment industry. High demand for drones has recently developed in a slightly unexpected market, the entertainment industry, where the purpose of drones is to enhance performance.

Major live events such as concerts and sports broadcasting have embraced the use of drones to enhance the visual effects for the audience. As drone technology keeps getting better, we can look forward to more creative and amazing uses of drones in media and entertainment.

Chapter 5 – Big Data

This chapter presents an overview of the state of the art of big data in the media and entertainment industry. We are living in the era of big data, which is huge amounts of data in digital form. For the media and entertainment industry, their customers are the real kings and big data is helping them to treat their customers like kings. The industry is experiencing a significant transformation with the integration of big data and analytics. Big data and analytics are key drivers for industry growth, extending beyond content personalization to strategic decision-making and significantly influencing the entertainment sector's overall success.

Chapter 6 – Cloud Computing

This chapter examines the various roles of cloud computing in the media and entertainment sector. Cloud computing has become a game-changer, offering seamless access to data anytime, anywhere. It has significantly impacted the media and entertainment industry, offering solutions for content creation, distribution, and management. In the media, cloud computing allows new ways of creating, managing, and broadcasting media content more effectively. M&E companies are increasingly eyeing the cloud platform to achieve their production, distribution, and archiving goals.

Chapter 7 – Blockchain

In this chapter, we will understand the potential of blockchain for media and entertainment. Blockchain is a digital, decentralized method of chronologically recording transactions in real-time that was originally developed to enable the concept of cryptocurrency, specifically Bitcoin, over a decade ago. Blockchain technology is transforming media and entertainment by reducing piracy, increasing transparency, connecting artists directly with fans, and verifying scarcity of digital collectibles. It is emerging as a critical tool in combatting fraud and enhancing transparency in digital advertising.

Chapter 8 – Immersive Technologies

This chapter examines the integration of immersive technology in the media and entertainment industry. Immersive technology aims to transport users to virtual environments or enhance their real-world experiences by overlaying digital information onto their physical surroundings. Based on technology, the immersive entertainment market is segmented into virtual reality (VR), augmented reality (AR), mixed reality (XR), and others. Immersive technologies are revolutionizing the media and entertainment industry by creating highly engaging and interactive experiences. From VR experiences to interactive storytelling, immersive technologies have the potential to redefine entertainment.

Chapter 9 – 5G Network

This chapter explores several applications of 5G in the media and entertainment industry. 5G network can bring fundamental changes to the entertainment broadcasting industry. It is set to revolutionize the media and entertainment industry by enabling faster data transfer speeds and lower latency, leading to enhanced streaming quality, immersive experiences, and new content creation possibilities. It shows great promise in solving several issues on both the production and consumption end of media and entertainment. It will drive the proliferation of richer entertainment, media, and advertising experiences.

Chapter 10 – Biometrics

This chapter examines various uses of biometrics in media and entertainment. Biometrics refer to the unique physical characteristics of a person, which could include fingerprints or facial recognition information. Biometrics, like fingerprints, facial recognition, and retinal scans, are increasingly used in the media and entertainment industry for a variety of purposes, including enhancing security, streamlining user experiences, and personalizing content. Advancements in biometrics will likely open up even more opportunities for innovation in the entertainment industry.

This book is a comprehensive text on the emerging technologies in the media and entertainment industry. It provides an overview of each emerging technology in a way that beginners can understand. It is a must-read for those interested in media and entertainment and its future.

I am grateful for the support of Dr. Annamalia Annamalai, the department head of the Department of Electrical and Computer Engineering, and Dr. Pamela Obiomon, the dean of the College of Engineering at Prairie View A&M University, Prairie View, Texas. Special thanks are due to my wife Dr. Janet Sadiku for helping in various ways. This book is dedicated to her.

- M. N. O. Sadiku, Westlake, FL

ABOUT THE AUTHOR

Matthew N. O. Sadiku received his B. Sc. degree in 1978 from Ahmadu Bello University, Zaria, Nigeria and his M.Sc. and Ph.D. degrees from Tennessee Technological University, Cookeville, TN in 1982 and 1984 respectively. From 1984 to 1988, he was an assistant professor at Florida Atlantic University, Boca Raton, FL, where he did graduate work in computer science. In total, he received seven college degrees. From 1988 to 2000, he was at Temple University, Philadelphia, PA, where he became a full professor. From 2000 to 2002, he was with Lucent/Avaya, Holmdel, NJ as a system engineer and with Boeing Satellite Systems, Los Angeles, CA as a senior scientist. He is presently a Regents professor emeritus of electrical and computer engineering at Prairie View A&M University, Prairie View, TX.

He is the author of over 1,460 professional papers and over 150 books including "Elements of Electromagnetics" (Oxford University Press, 7th ed., 2018), "Fundamentals of Electric Circuits" (McGraw-Hill, 7th ed., 2020, with C. Alexander), "Computational Electromagnetics with MATLAB" (CRC Press, 4th ed., 2019), "Principles of Modern Communication Systems" (Cambridge University Press, 2017, with S. O. Agbo), and "Emerging Internet-based Technologies" (CRC Press, 2019). In addition to the engineering books, he has written Christian books including "Secrets of Successful Marriages" (with J. O. Sadiku), "How to Discover God's Will for Your Life," and commentaries on all the books of the New Testament Bible. Some of his books have been translated into ten languages: French, Korean, Chinese (and Chinese Long Form in Taiwan), Italian, Portuguese, Spanish, German, Dutch, Polish, and Russian.

He was the recipient of the 2000 McGraw-Hill/Jacob Millman Award for outstanding contributions in the field of electrical engineering. He was also the recipient of Regents Professor award for 2012-2013 by the Texas A&M University System. He is a registered professional engineer and a life fellow of the Institute of Electrical and Electronics Engineers (IEEE) "for contributions to computational electromagnetics and engineering education." He was the IEEE Region 2 Student Activities Committee Chairman. He was an associate editor for IEEE Transactions on Education. He is also a member of Association for Computing Machinery (ACM). His current research interests are in the areas of computational electromagnetic, computer science/networks, engineering education, and marriage counseling. His works can be found in his autobiography, "My Life and Work" (Trafford Publishing, 2024) or his website: www.matthew-sadiku.com. He can be reached via email at sadiku@ieee.org

TABLE OF CONTENTS

CHAPTER 1
INTRODUCTION

"Entertainment is temporary happiness, but the real happiness is permanent entertainment."

— Anonymous

1.1 INTRODUCTION

Earlier, people used to spend their quality time with their friends and family sitting around the campfire. Today, with rapid advancement in technology, the television had become a main base of entertainment. The media and entertainment industry is undergoing a significant transformation, driven by emerging technologies that are redefining how content is created, delivered, and consumed. Media technology like artificial intelligence (AI)-powered automation in content creation are improving efficiency and audience engagement. The emerging technologies continue to reshape the way we live, work, and interact. By harnessing emerging technologies, media companies can deliver tailored content and craft interactive environments that cater to individual preferences.

The media and entertainment industry is driven by technology. Technology innovations are transforming the media and entertainment (M&E) industry, affecting every aspect from content creation to distribution and consumption. It is evident that technology has a central role to play in the business of entertainment media and technologies in determining the kind of content that is produced. The role of media and entertainment distributors in this transformation cannot be overstated, as they connect creators with their audiences and adapt to the ever-evolving technological landscape [1]. Figure 1.1 shows a representation of entertainment

[2].

Figure 1.1 A representation of entertainment [2].

Technology has been the main driving factor for the media and entertainment (M&E) industry and it is modernizing the industry. The M&E industry continues to rapidly evolve and transform. New media technologies are changing the game and shaping content creation, distribution, and consumption. The M&E industry is undergoing significant transformations that will impact the future of television. Social media applications like YouTube, TikTok, and Instagram have become primary distribution channels that allow content creators to get to millions of people at first. This democratization is not devoid of its problems for the same reason – namely, the rapidly growing number of media products, it becomes practically impossible for each media product to be noticeable [3].

This chapter looks at the top emerging technologies in the media and entertainment industry. It begins with explaining emerging technologies. It briefly covers some emerging technologies in the media and entertainment industry. It highlights the benefits and challenges of emerging technologies in media and entertainment. The last section concludes with comments.

1.2 WHAT ARE EMERGING TECHNOLOGIES?

Technology may be regarded as a collection of systems designed to perform some function. It can help alleviate some of the challenges facing business today. Emerging technology is a term generally used to describe new technology. The term often refers to technologies currently developing or expected to be available within the next five to ten years. Any imminent, but not fully realized, technological innovations will have some impact on the status quo.

Emerging technologies are shaping our societies. They continue to affect the way we live, work, and interact with one another. Emerging technology (ET) lacks a consensus on what classifies them as "emergent." It is a relative term because one may see a technology as emerging and others may not see it the same way. It is a term that is often used to describe a new technology. A technology is still emerging if it is not yet a "must-have" [4]. An emerging technology is the one that holds the promise of creating a new economic engine and is trans-industrial. ET is used in different areas such as media, healthcare, business, science, education, or defense.

The characteristics of emerging technologies include the following [5]:

- *Novelty:* Emerging technologies are typically new or novel, meaning they have yet to be widely adopted or used. They often represent a significant departure from existing technologies or processes.

- *Potential for Disruption:* Emerging technologies have the potential to disrupt existing markets, industries, or ways of doing things. They may also displace existing businesses or industries.

- *Uncertainty:* Because emerging technologies are still in the early stages of development, there is often a high uncertainty surrounding their future potential and impact. It can be challenging to predict how they will evolve.

- *Rapid Change:* Emerging technologies often evolve rapidly, with new developments and innovations emerging frequently. It can make keeping up with the latest trends and advancements challenging.

- *Interdisciplinary:* Emerging technologies often involve multiple disciplines or fields of study, such as computer science, engineering, and biology. They may require collaboration across different fields and industries to develop their potential fully.

Emerging technologies are worth investigating. They are responsible for developing new products or devices. As emerging technologies continue to evolve, engineering is poised for a transformative future. Emerging technologies have driven innovation and progress in today's rapidly evolving digital landscape. The collective impact of emerging technologies such as artificial intelligence, machine learning, big data, and the Internet of things is undeniably transformative. Some emerging technologies are shown in Figure 1.2 [6].

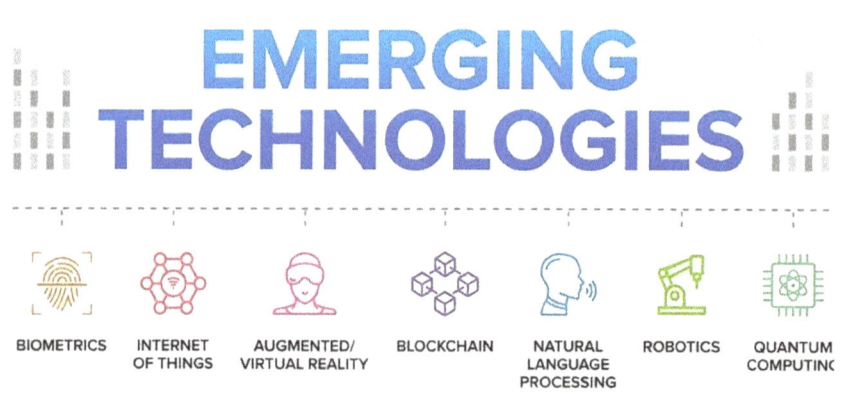

Figure 1.2 Some emerging technologies [6]

1.3 EMERGING TECHNOLOGIES IN MEDIA & ENTERTAINMENT

Technology plays an incredible role in the media and entertainment. Several key technologies are set to have a major impact on the media and entertainment industry. These include the following [7-9]:

1. *Artificial Intelligence:* Within the M&E industry, AI's three most important functions will be recommendation, voice recognition, and media automation. AI enables media companies to deliver hyper-personalized content and adapt to shifting experiences to individual viewer preferences. AI is being used to personalize content recommendations, generate media, and improve the user experience. It is poised to revolutionize content production and consumption. By automating tasks, analyzing viewer preferences, and generating curated recommendations, AI and machine learning will empower media companies to deliver bespoke experiences that truly resonate with viewers. As demand for content localization increases, AI automates the translation and adaptation of media for global audiences. Companies will double-down on GenAI to accelerate content production, facilitate more efficient content distribution, scale personalized marketing efforts, and bolster monetization. Figure 1.3 shows a representation of AI [7]. As shown in Figure 1.4, Disney has formed business unit to utilize AI and AR [10].

Figure 1.3 A representation of AI [7]

Figure 1.4 Disney has formed business unit to utilize AI and AR [10]

2.   *Robotics:* Robotics drives a shift toward precision, efficiency, and enhanced creativity in media industry. It gives opportunities for automation in complex, large-scale media environments that require huge reliance on human labor. Robotics boosts operational efficiency, reduces costs, and ensures reliable media production. Robotic camera arms and drone automation are used in filming, particularly in complex or dangerous environments.

3. *Drones:* With the emergence of drone technology, impressive photography and aerial filming has become possible. Drones help you to capture breath-taking scenes from different angles. They enable you to acquire the details of inaccessible locations and make detailed documentation. They have become an indispensable unit in the entertainment industry and benefits with great cost savings.

4. *Cloud Computing:* The use of cloud-native technologies has become ubiquitous in the video industry. Media companies leverage cloud computing to handle data-heavy workflows like AI-driven content creation and predictive analytics. Cloud computing offers computational power to process large datasets. It also enables real-time analytics for ad campaigns to allow advertisers to track performance metrics such as viewer engagement and click-through rate.

5. *Big Data:* Big data and analytics significantly improve customer satisfaction to ensure longer viewing sessions and higher retention rates. Advanced data analytics allows media businesses to predict shows or movies in demand. Big data and analytics thus empower media companies to understand audience engagement and advertising effectiveness at a much deeper level. They measure ad campaign effectiveness across platforms using attribution modeling and data segmentation. Big data will remain the primary tool for creating highly personalized experiences that go beyond simple content recommendations as media consumption becomes more dispersed.

6. *Blockchain:* Blockchain solves long-standing concerns about piracy, sharing revenue, and content ownership. It verifies ad impressions and engagement to combat ad fraud. It provides transparency and trust in ad spending to ensure real viewers see ads. Blockchain secures intellectual property and tracks content ownership through smart contracts and distributed ledgers. The technology has the potential to secure digital content and protect intellectual property. For example, blockchain could be used to create secure and transparent platforms for content distribution, or to ensure that authors and artists receive proper compensation

for their work. Blockchain technology has introduced a new era in handling digital ownership through the introduction of non-fungible tokens (NFTs). Unlike traditional tickets, NFTs can be programmed to include additional perks such as VIP experiences, exclusive content access, or the ability to resell tickets on secondary markets. Blockchain and NFTs are poised to reshape digital asset ownership and fan engagement. Nigerian startup Dramebase develops a blockchain-based decentralized media streaming platform, while Belgian startup PlayTreks develops a blockchain-based music distribution marketplace.

7. *Internet of Things:* IoT devices assist media companies in understanding consumer behavior, enhancing real-time personalization, and improving operational efficiency by enabling real-time data collection and, in turn, analysis. IoT enhances audience interaction and enables more innovative and responsive media services.

8. *Immersive Technology:* Emerging technologies in media and entertainment include virtual reality (VR), augmented reality (AR), mixed reality (MR), and the metaverse, which are transforming how we experience content and interact with digital worlds. These technologies offer 3D environments and virtual space to enable immersive storytelling and interactive content capabilities. They provide immersive experiences, redefine viewer engagement, and create new opportunities for content creation and distribution. They will continue to redefine how we experience media and entertainment. VR can be used for virtual concerts, gaming, and movie-going experiences, while AR allows for overlaid digital content onto the real world, and MR blends both. The metaverse is being explored for entertainment, social interaction, and even e-commerce. Figure 1.5 is an example of immersive experience [7].

Figure 1.5 An example of immersive experience [7].

9. *5G Network:* Connectivity is moving outside of the tethered cell phone to direct connected 5G-enabled high end IoT devices, the still camera, video camera, televisions, over the top playout devices, health wearables, real-time coaching, and many more that will come to market. Connectivity technologies solve long-standing issues like latency, bandwidth constraints, and fragmented distribution. 5G's incredible speeds and low latency will usher in a new era of individualized experiences. From real-time interactions and personalized content to extended reality (XR) applications that blend the physical and digital worlds, 5G will reshape audience engagement with content. It is expected to fuel innovations in autonomous vehicles, smart cities, and the Internet of things (IoT) with near-instantaneous data transmission, paving the way for real-time communication between devices. China Unicom & Huawei launched the world's first large-scale integrated 5G-Advanced intelligent network. Figure 1.6 shows a representation of 5G [7].

Figure 1.6 A representation of 5G [7]

10. *Biometrics:* Biometrics improves content verification and personalized user interaction in the media sector. These technologies allow media companies to secure the integrity of their content by verifying the source and authorship of media like videos and images. Biometrics also safeguard digital media assets from piracy as well as find applications in content protection, targeted advertising, and subscription management.

Other emerging technologies include metaverse, clean tech, web 3, 3D printing, edge computing, and quantum computing.

1.4 BENEFITS

Emerging technologies can deliver tailored content and craft interactive environments that cater to individual preferences. The shifts in consumer behavior are not only redefining the media and entertainment industry; they are setting the stage for a new era of digital consumption, where personalization, interactivity, and multi-platform accessibility are key. Success lies in technical proficiency and understanding the pulse of consumer expectations. Other benefits of emerging technologies in media and entertainment include the following [2,11]:

• *Personalization:* There is a growing preference for personalized, on-demand content driven by advancements in AI and machine learning. Consumers now expect media that caters to their tastes and schedules moving away from traditional, scheduled programming. Integrating AI in content personalization is not just a trend; it is a revolution reshaping the media and entertainment landscape. Globally, AI is reshaping how content is curated and consumed, offering viewers a more immersive, personalized experience. Gen AI will play a crucial role in personalized content suggestions, handling shopping queries, productizing content recommendations, facilitating interactive advertising, and addressing cybersecurity threats. Figure 1.7 shows a representation of personalization [12].

Figure 1.7 A representation of personalization [12]

• *Interactive Experiences:* The demand for interactive content, such as virtual reality and augmented reality experiences, is on the rise. Interactive and immersive experiences are driving a profound transformation in the media and entertainment industry. Consumers increasingly seek more engaging and participatory content in a shifting media landscape. They seek more than passive viewing; they want engaging, immersive experiences that blur the lines between viewer and content. Interactive shopping will find its place on the TV, blurring the boundary between content consumption and e-commerce.

• *Automation:* AI is already being used to automate many aspects of media production, from content creation and distribution to analysis and recommendation. Language models are propelling AI into realms beyond our initial expectations, automating tasks like extensive dataset analysis and amplifying productivity for providers of video services. AI-powered voice assistants like Siri and Alexa are becoming increasingly popular, allowing users to interact with media content using voice commands. Figure 1.8 shows an example of automation [13].

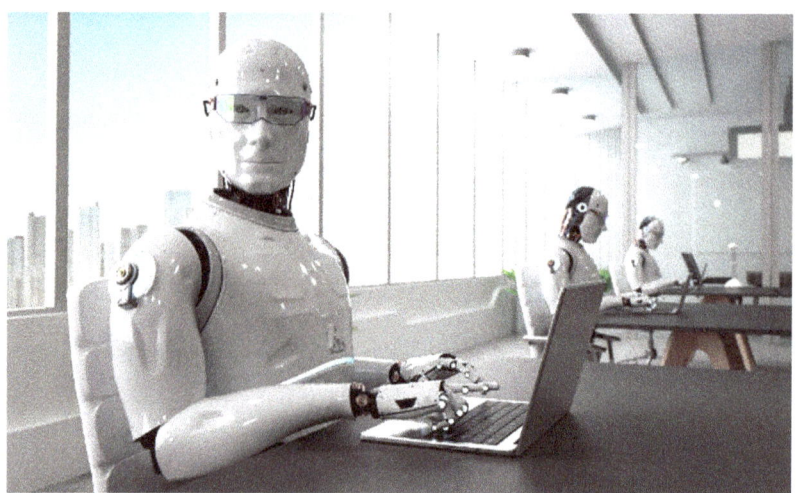

Figure 1.8 An example of Automation [13]

• *Social Media:* Social media has evolved into a massive, unified distribution platform, making immediate global reach highly feasible for both brands and creators. Short-form videos on TikTok and Instagram Reels are becoming a medium of choice to reach younger demographics, while YouTube remains strong for longer-form and educational content. People still want the TV and movie experience offered by traditional studios, but social platforms are becoming competitive for their entertainment time. Social platforms can also make it easy for advertisers to buy ads and target specific cohorts with clear results. Figure 1.9 shows a representation of social media [14].

Figure 1.9 A representation of social media [14]

• *Gamification:* Interactive content and gamification are revolutionizing brand interaction with audiences. Gamification incorporates game-like elements that reward users with points, badges, and leaderboards. Such elements encourage users to get more involved and stay for longer stretches. When applied well, gamified experiences build community. Experts predict that the gaming industry will follow a similar trajectory to other digital technologies such as social media, mobile apps, and e-commerce. Figure 1.10 shows an example of gamification [14].

Figure 1.10 An example of gamification [14].

• *Advertising:* Today's advertisers have figured out that context is king. This has paved the way for a contextual media gold rush where advertisements are selected and served by automated systems based on the context of what a user is looking at. Apart from encouraging user engagement, contextual media also has the advantage of not disrupting the viewing experience significantly. Pre-rolls, in-stream, and post-roll ads have already proven their effectiveness in increasing the monetization for distributors. The deep insights available through a modern video ad server enable advertisers to serve customized ads to different consumers during the same stream. AI will also help advertisers in narrowing down on ads that will capture the viewer's attention and will not interfere with the visual experience. Figure 1.11 shows a representation of advertising [12].

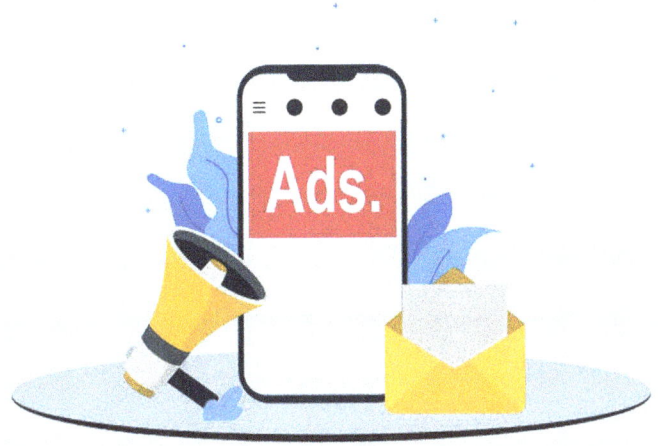

Figure 1.11 A representation of advertising [13].

1.5 CHALLENGES

There are potential challenges and ethical considerations associated with emerging technologies. These must be addressed in order for widespread adoption to take place.

For example, there are concerns about the potential impact of VR on mental health, as well as issues related to data privacy and security in the use of AI. There are also concerns about the potential for these technologies to reinforce existing biases or perpetuate harmful stereotypes. Service cancellations are problematic for streaming video on-demand companies that have been dependent on subscription revenues to support their costs. Other challenges of emerging technologies in media and entertainment include the following [15]:

• *Risk:* As AI adoption gains momentum across the industry and companies seek to maximize their AI advantage, they will also need to establish proper risk governance and controls, including fair use, safety, copyright norms, and talent compensation. For example, there is the risk of AI-generated content being used to spread misinformation or propaganda, or of AI algorithms being used to manipulate public opinion.

- *Costs:* Costs and risk have narrowed cinema to very expensive and safe franchises. The rising service costs and widespread price sensitivities may be contributing to persistent and high churn rates among consumers. The costs of producing and distributing TV and films continue to go up, while the revenue they generate has gone down.

- *Sustainability:* Sustainability is becoming a priority in media production. There is an increasing trend in adopting sustainable production methods within the media and entertainment industry. It is driven by the growing consumer demand for greener working methods and climate change. The media and entertainment industry will see a heightened focus on sustainability. As digital consumption increases, some platforms are also considering their environmental impact, looking at ways to reduce digital carbon footprints and promote sustainable viewing habits.

- *Interoperability:* Media and entertainment companies are increasingly pushing for an interoperable digital space where users can socialize, attend virtual concerts, and participate in interactive storytelling experiences.

- *Cybersecurity:* Cybersecurity threats are on the rise. As technology evolves, so do cybersecurity threats. Ransomware attacks, in particular, have surged, with cybercriminals targeting hospitals, schools, and government institutions. Aside from cybersecurity threats, the M&E industry will also need to consider the potential harm of deepfakes, and the impact that pirates could have on a studio's business.

1.6 CONCLUSION

The media and entertainment industry is currently transforming, primarily fueled by the advent of groundbreaking technologies. AI, generative AI, and augmented reality (AR) are at the forefront of this revolution. For example, AI and Gen AI are revolutionizing content personalization and creation. AR offers immersive experiences that blend digital elements with the real world. TV streaming services such as Netflix, Hulu, and Disney plus are among the leading service providers of movies, TV shows, and documentaries to consumers. This change from cable television to streaming has upended conventional business models as well as creating new opportunities for companies that are willing to take the risks. Leaders such as IBM, Nvidia, Google, Microsoft, and OpenAI drive emerging technologies across the world whilst tackling ethical concerns and regulations.

Emerging technologies are undoubtedly transforming the media landscape and offering new opportunities for creativity and innovation. These technologies are opening up new possibilities for storytelling, entertainment, education, and even social engagement. The future of media and entertainment is being shaped by rapid technological advancements.

More information about emerging technologies in the media and entertainment industry can be found in this related journal: *Journal on Emerging Technologies.*

REFERENCES

[1] "How technology is revolutionizing the media and entertainment industry," November 2023,

https://www.arkinfo.in/blog/how-technology-is-revolutionizing-the-media-and-entertainment-industry

[2] S. Sajdak, "Current trends in media and entertainment industry: Guide for 2024," January 2024,

https://www.miquido.com/blog/trends-in-media-and-entertainment/

[3] M. N. O. Sadiku, P. A. Adekunte, and J. O. Sadiku, "Emerging technologies in media and entertainment," *International Journal of Trend in Scientific Research and Development*, vol. 9, no. 3, May-June 2025, pp. 331-339.

[4] M. Halaweh, "Emerging technology: What is it?" *Journal of Technology Management & Innovation*, vol. 8, no. 3, 2013, pp. 108-115.

[5] N. Duggal, "Top 18 new technology trends for 2023," July 2023,

https://www.simplilearn.com/top-technology-trends-and-jobs-article

[6] "How enterprise architects integrate emerging technologies to enhance architecture,"

https://www.linkedin.com/pulse/how-enterprise-architects-integrate-emerging-technologies-qdgfe/

[7] J. Arensberg, "The future of media and entertainment: How emerging tech will reshape the industry," January 2025,

https://www.tvtechnology.com/opinion/the-future-of-media-and-entertainment-how-emerging-tech-will-reshape-the-industry

[8] "The next wave of media technology: 10 emerging technologies,"

https://www.startus-insights.com/innovators-guide/media-technology/

[9] K. Panchal, "Top 10 emerging technology trends for entertainment industry," January 2021,

https://www.ifourtechnolab.com/blog/top-10-emerging-technology-trends-for-entertainment-industry

[10] K. Wheeler, "Top 10: Emerging technologies," January 2025,

https://technologymagazine.com/articles/top-10-emerging-technologies

[11] "4 emerging trends and challenges shaping the future of the media industry," March 2020,

https://www.nagarro.com/en/blog/emerging-trends-shaping-future-media-industry

[12] " Emerging trends in media & entertainment industry,"

https://www.prologic-technologies.com/blog/emerging-trends-in-media-entertainment-industry

[13] "Top technology trends in media and entertainment industry that you should consider,"

https://ocnjdaily.com/news/2024/jun/22/top-technology-trends-in-media-and-entertainment-i/

[14] "The changing face of media and entertainment: Trends to follow in 2025," October 2024,

https://www.avenga.com/magazine/trends-in-the-media-and-entertainment-industry/

[15] A. Nochimowski, "Technology trends reshaping media & entertainment in 2024," February 2024,

https://www.thefastmode.com/expert-opinion/34850-technology-trends-reshaping-media-entertainment-in-2024

CHAPTER 2
ARTIFICIAL INTELLIGENCE IN MEDIA AND ENTERTAINMENT

*"What do you actually need? Food, clothing and shelter.
Everything else is entertainment."*

— Aloe Blacc

2.1 INTRODUCTION

The media and entertainment (M&E) industry is diverse and quite complex, including sectors such as movies, gaming, advertising, music, sports, content creation, etc. The boundaries between these segments are becoming less distinct, but they all share one common goal: providing captivating content that can be monetized. The M&E industry is centered around innovation and attracting audiences with amazing technologies. It is crucial for both creators and audiences to recognize the media's strong influence in shaping our views, values, and culture. Figure 2.1 represents the M&E industry [1].

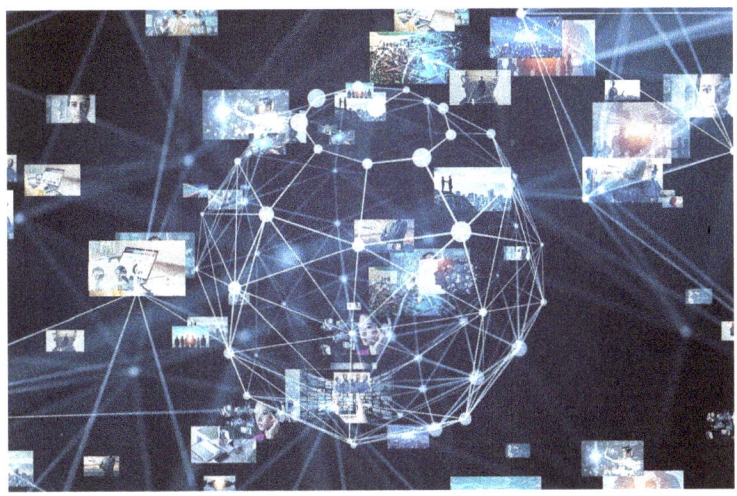

Figure 2.1 A representation of the M&E industry [1].

In this technological evolving world, we must adopt the latest technologies to boost success. And for the media and entertainment industry, AI is the best option. Artificial intelligence (AI) has impacted various industries, and media and entertainment are no exception. The use of AI in the media and entertainment industry has augmented and improved user experiences and has played an influential role in how content is made and delivered to users. AI has subtly but powerfully reshaped our media and entertainment experiences. The key benefit of integrating artificial intelligence into the entertainment and media industry is its ability to efficiently analyze large amounts of data. Moreover, AI emphasizes the simplicity by solving complaints in the best way, making the discovery and automated of routine works [2].

From automating creative processes to enhancing audience engagement, AI is revolutionizing entertainment by transforming how content is created, personalized, and experienced. AI is powering a new generation of software tools and technologies that is already changing how M&E companies create and distribute content, manage operations, and make sense of data. AI is extensively used in entertainment platforms such as YouTube, Netflix, and Amazon Prime Video to provide personalized recommendations to users.

The media and entertainment industry has always been a hub of innovation, captivating audiences with groundbreaking technologies. Now, artificial intelligence (AI) is taking these boundaries even further. AI has so much potential to transform the media and entertainment industry. It offers tools like predictive analytics, recommendation engines, customer journey mapping, and audience segmentation. AI may be regarded as a blockbuster force dramatically altering content creation, distribution, and consumption in the media and entertainment industry [3].

In this chapter, we will explore some popular use cases of artificial intelligence (AI) in the media and entertainment industry. The chapter begins with explaining AI and generative AI. It describes AI in media and entertainment and presents some examples. It provides some applications of AI in the media and entertainment industry. It highlights the benefits and challenges of AI in media and entertainment. The last section concludes with comments.

2.2 WHAT IS ARTIFICIAL INTELLIGENCE?

The term "artificial intelligence" (AI) is an umbrella term John McCarthy, a computer scientist, coined in 1955 and de-fined as "the science and engineering of in-telligent machines." It refers to the ability of a computer system to perform human tasks (such as thinking and learning) that usually can only be accomplished using human intelligence [4]. Typically, AI systems demonstrate at least some of the following human behaviors: planning, learning, reasoning, problem solving, knowledge representation, perception, speech recognition, decision-making, language translation, motion, manipulation, intelligence, and creativity.

The 10 U.S. Code § 2358 define artificial intelligence as [5]:

"Any artificial system that performs tasks under varying and unpredictable circumstances without significant human oversight, or that can learn from experience and improve performance when exposed to data sets.

1. An artificial system developed in computer software, physical hardware, or other context that solves tasks requiring

human-like perception, cognition, planning, learning, communication, or physical action.

2. An artificial system designed to think or act like a human, including cognitive architectures and neural networks.

3. A set of techniques, including machine learning, that is designed to approximate a cognitive task.

4. An artificial system designed to act rationally, including an intelligent software agent or embodied robot that achieves goals using perception, planning, reasoning, learning, communicating, decision making, and acting."

AI provides tools creating intelligent machines which can behave like humans, think like humans, and make decisions like humans. The main goals of artificial intelligence are [6]:

1. Replicate human intelligence

2. Solve knowledge-intensive tasks

3. Make an intelligent connection of perception and action

4. Build a machine which can perform tasks that requires human intelligence

Create some system which can exhibit intelligent behavior, learn new things by itself, demonstrate, explain, and can advise to its user.

AI is not a single technology but a range of computational models and algorithms. The concept of AI is an umbrella term that encompasses many different technologies. AI is not a single technology but a collection of techniques that enables computer systems to perform tasks that would otherwise require human intelligence. The major disciplines in AI include [7]:

- *Expert systems*

- *Fuzzy logic*

- *Neural networks*

- *Machine learning (ML)*

- *Deep learning*

- *Natural Language Processors (NLP)*

- *Robots*

These computer-based tools or technologies have been used to achieve AI's goals. Each AI tool has its own advantages. Using a combination of these models, rather than a single model, is recommended. Figure 2.2 shows a typical expert system, while 2. 3 illustrates the AI tools. These tools are gaining momentum across every industry. Analytics can be considered a core AI capability.

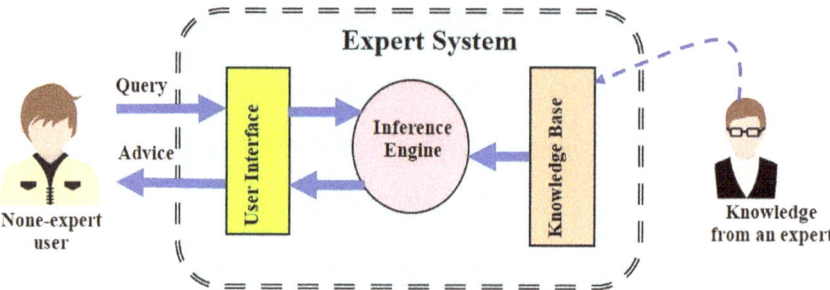

Figure 2.2 A typical expert system.

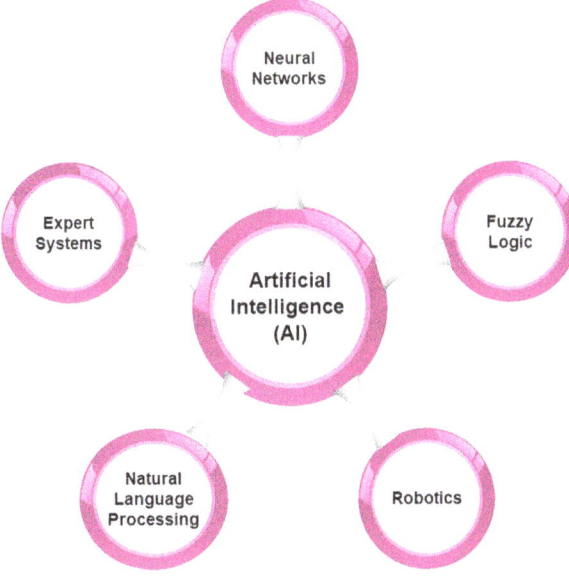

Figure 2.3 AI tools.

2.3 GENERATIVE AI

Artificial Intelligence (AI) is increasingly a part of our world and it is rapidly changing our lives. Generative AI (GenAI) is a subset of artificial intelligence that uses generative models to produce text, images, videos, or other forms of data. Generative AI (GenAI) is a term for any type of AI system capable of using generative models to create new forms of humanlike creative content, like text, images, music, audio, video and more. GenAI models include various algorithms able to learn the various patterns and structures of input training data before generating novel outputs with similar characteristics. It is essentially a narrow type and application of the broader artificial intelligence umbrella of technologies. It describes algorithms (such as ChatGPT) that can be used to create new content, including audio, code, images, text, simulations, and videos. It is specifically designed and trained to generate new content. The versatility and potential of GenAI to transform various aspects of business operations make it an attractive investment for companies across industries. GenAI uses neural networks, machine learning, deep learning models, complex algorithms, and large and varied training datasets to produce original content based on user input and how to reason in ways akin to a human brain. The technology is built on AI tools shown in Figure 2.4 [8]. It uses neural networks to identify the patterns and structures within existing data to generate new and original content.

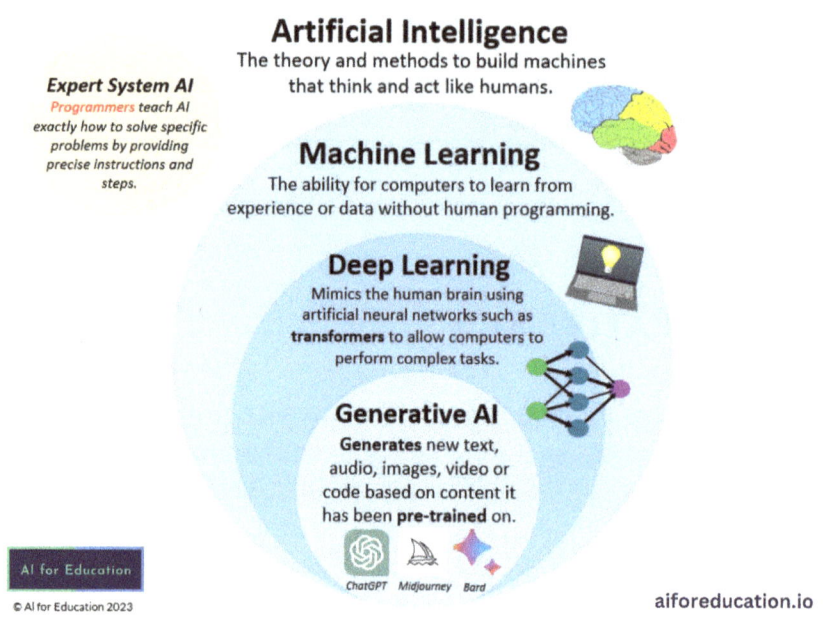

Figure 2.4 GenAI built on AI tools listed above [8].

Generative AI can be thought of as a machine-learning model that is trained to create new data, rather than making a prediction about a specific dataset. Since its inception, the field of machine learning used both discriminative models and generative models, to model and predict data. A generative AI system is constructed by applying unsupervised machine learning or self-supervised machine learning to a data set. The most common way to train a generative AI model is to use supervised learning. Generative AI can also be trained on the motions of a robotic system to generate new trajectories for motion planning or navigation. Generative AI models are used to power chatbot products such as ChatGPT [9].

Generative AI is transforming nearly all aspects of the pharmaceutical industry, revamping the way companies operate and potentially unlocking billions of dollars in value. The pharmaceutical-operations value chain encompasses sourcing, manufacturing, quality, and the supply chain—and gen AI is expected to improve them all

2.4 AI IN MEDIA AND ENTERTAINMENT

The media and entertainment industry is undergoing a seismic shift, driven by the relentless advancement of technology. The entertainment industry constantly evolves and adapts to new technologies and consumer demands. One of the biggest trends expected to shape the industry is artificial intelligence (AI). One of the most significant ways AI influences the media and entertainment industry is by adeptly customizing content and experiences to suit individual consumers. AI in entertainment means the application of AI technology in the media and entertainment sector for better content creation, distribution, and personalization.

Today, AI plays a crucial role in the media and entertainment industry, from how content is created, disseminated, and appreciated to tailored suggestions to content generation. The impact of AI in media and entertainment industry has been significant, with many companies utilizing AI to improve their operations, enhance the consumer experience, and create more personalized content. Various entertainment industries using AI are virtual reality, games, movies, TV shows, music, and social media. Figure 2.5 represents AI in media and entertainment [10].

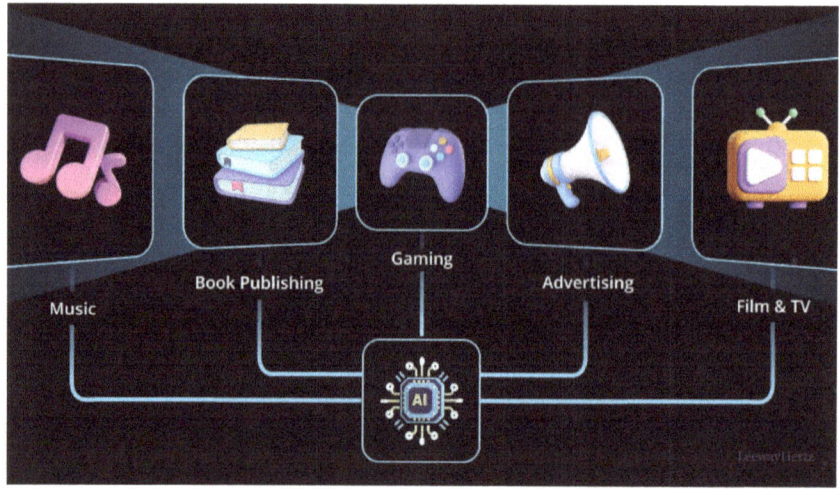

Figure 2.5 AI in media and entertainment [10].

The integration of AI into the entertainment industry is revolutionizing content creation, personalization, and audience engagement. The rise of AI in entertainment has led to an unprecedented reliance on vast amounts of personal, behavioral, and proprietary data, raising concerns about privacy, security, and ownership. Whether in film, television, gaming, or social media, AI has introduced new capabilities that enhance creative workflows and streamline production.

2.5 EXAMPLES OF AI IN THE ENTERTAINMENT AND MEDIA

The media and entertainment landscape is on the cusp of a radical transformation driven by the relentless advancement of artificial intelligence. From revolutionizing content creation and personalization to automating workflows and generating new revenue streams, artificial intelligence in media is transforming the industry. Presence of AI in media and entertainment industry is showcased through a range of practical instances. The following real-world examples illustrate this trend [10-12]:

• *Netflix:* Neflix's recommendation system is powered by AI algorithms, which analyze user data to provide tailored content suggestions, leading to longer user engagement. Machine Learning in entertainment powers Netflix's recommendation engine, learning from user viewing habits and preferences. AI in media & entertainment is a key driver of Netflix's success.

• *Spotify:* Spotify's music recommendation system employs AI to suggest tracks that match the listener's taste or habits, and it is so accurate that it almost feels like a personalized DJ. Machine Learning in entertainment analyzes user music preferences to generate custom playlists. AI in media and entertainment is transforming how people discover and enjoy music.

• *Adobe:* Adobe Sensei uses AI to power various features in Adobe Creative Cloud applications, such as content-aware fill and facial recognition. AI-driven innovations in film and television rely on Adobe Sensei for various creative tasks. Artificial Intelligence in media is empowering creative professionals with powerful tools.

• *IBM Watson:* This is used in various media and entertainment applications, such as script analysis and content creation. AI-driven media solutions leverage IBM Watson's cognitive computing capabilities. AI in media & entertainment is exploring new frontiers in content creation and analysis.

• *Google's AI-powered Translation:* These translation tools are used to translate subtitles and dub content for different languages. AI-driven media solutions enable efficient and accurate content localization. AI in media and entertainment is breaking down language barriers and connecting global audiences.

• *Scriptbook:* Scriptbook is an AI-powered script analysis tool used by film studios to predict the commercial success of a screenplay. The tool analyzes the script's characters, themes, and plot points and then compares this data to the performance of similar films in the past to predict box office success.

• *AIVA:* AIVA (Artificial Intelligence Virtual Artist) is an AI-powered music composition tool that can create original music tracks based on user preferences. The tool analyzes data points such as genre, tempo, and mood to create unique compositions that can be used in films, TV shows, and video games.

• *DeepMotion:* DeepMotion is an AI-powered animation tool that can create realistic 3D animations for video games and films. The tool uses machine learning algorithms to simulate human movement and behavior, allowing for more realistic and natural-looking animations.

• *Ziva:* Ziva Dynamics is an AI-powered software tool for creating realistic 3D character models for films and video games. The tool uses machine learning algorithms to simulate the movement of muscles and skin, allowing for more realistic and detailed character models.

• *LyricFind:* LyricFind is a lyrics search engine driven by AI, enabling users to find song lyrics by using everyday language queries. The system employs natural language processing algorithms to comprehend user queries and deliver precise and fitting outcomes.

2.6 APPLICATIONS OF AI IN MEDIA AND ENTERTAINMENT

AI is seamlessly weaving its magic across the vibrant landscape of the media and entertainment industry, notably revitalizing diverse domains such as music, film and TV, gaming, advertising, book publishing, and content creation. Media and entertainment industries are using AI to enhancing the rate, affordability, and simplicity of content production, management, distribution, and consumption. AI's value is evident in content creation, game development, targeted marketing and advertising, music analysis, and real-time streaming. Some applications of AI in M&E industry are shown in Figure 2.6 [13]. Common applications of AI in M&E sector include the following [10,14]:

Applications of AI in Media and Entertainment Industry

Figure 2.6 Some applications of AI in M&E industry [13].

- *Content Creation:* AI impacts media and entertainment in the area of content creation. It generates articles, blogs, and scripts and assists in video and audio production, maintaining a consistent tone and style. Generative AI emerges as a game-changer by automating the generation of characters, animations, and visual effects customized for specific themes, genres, or formats. This technology not only enhances efficiency in content production but also ensures consistent quality and creativity. Customizing content and experiences to suit individual consumers is one of the critical influences of AI in the media and entertainment industry. Moreover, AI enhances content creation efficiency by automating tasks like video editing, proofreading, and even generating ad copy, resulting in cost reductions and heightened productivity. Big companies like YouTube use machine learning development algorithms to analyze viewing data and recommend content to users. Content production in the media and entertainment sectors is booming, thanks to the rise of influencers and creators on platforms like TikTok and Instagram. This approach allows Ubisoft to create expansive game worlds, generate realistic landscapes, and populate them with interactive elements while reducing the manual effort required for content creation. Figure 2.7 shows an example of AI-driven procedural content generation, Assassin's Creed Mirage by Ubisoft [15].

Figure 2.7 An example of AI-driven procedural content generation [15].

• *Video Production:* Personalized videos are transforming film and TV production, offering opportunities to feature individuals and iconic figures in unique ways. This innovation aims to streamline production costs and reduce staffing requirements in the entertainment industry. Generative AI plays a pivotal role in this transformation by generating personalized videos that incorporate individuals and iconic figures seamlessly. By leveraging AI-generated content, film and TV productions can achieve greater efficiency and creativity, ultimately offering viewers a more personalized and engaging viewing experience.

• *Advertising and Marketing:* AI is being used to improve marketing and advertising in the media and entertainment industry. By gathering data about consumer activities and patterns, AI algorithms enable companies to fine-tune promotional messages to target the target audience precisely. In advertising and marketing, the focus is on maximizing engagement and conversion rates through targeted campaigns. Businesses leverage AI to understand user data deeply, ensuring advertisements resonate effectively with their target audiences. AI-driven insights optimize ad placement, ensuring advertisements appear where they are most relevant and likely to drive meaningful user engagement. AI algorithms scrutinize user behavior and preferences to offer tailored advertisements across diverse digital platforms.

• *Interactive Storytelling:* Interactive storytelling challenges storytellers to create dynamic narratives that adapt based on audience choices, enhancing engagement and immersion in digital experiences. AI aids in storytelling by enhancing various aspects of content creation and delivery. Generative AI transforms interactive storytelling by enabling the creation of dynamic narratives that evolve in real-time based on audience interactions. By leveraging AI-driven capabilities, creators can innovate in gaming, digital entertainment, and educational platforms, offering audiences more engaging and participatory narratives that evolve dynamically with each interaction.

• *Music Analysis:* An advantage of AI in music production is its ability to personalize the listening experience. In music and audio analysis, businesses seek to enhance user experience through personalized music recommendations and improved audio quality. Generative AI enhances user engagement by suggesting music tracks and playlists tailored to individual preferences and listening histories. Streaming services like Spotify and Apple Music already employ AI algorithms to recommend songs based on a user's listening patterns, yet the technology can extend further. AI algorithms use machine learning to analyze vast datasets covering music genres, artists, lyrics, and user interactions. Through this process, they precisely forecast and deliver music that resonates with users' preferences, enriching their overall listening journey

• *Predictive Analytics:* Predictive analytics, driven by artificial intelligence, has emerged as the marketing game-changer, offering companies a competitive advantage. AI in media and entertainment is used in predictive analytics, using data, statistical algorithms, and machine learning techniques to forecast future outcomes based on historical data. Predictive AI algorithms can analyze viewer behavior, preferences and consumption patterns across massive sets of data. This can enable companies to harness the power of data via trained AI models to predict, plan and meet increasingly complex global audience demands. By leveraging predictive analytics, you can make informed decisions, refine your marketing strategies, and elevate your customers' experiences. Predictive analytics empowers advertisers to fine-tune their ad placements and timing, maximizing the effectiveness of their campaigns for better results.

• *Gaming:* The gaming industry is experiencing a revolution driven by AI advancements. AI enriches game design by enhancing non-player characters (NPCs) and refining game mechanics through its capability to create realistic and challenging behaviors, subsequently elevating the player's experience. AI algorithms excel at delivering personalized game suggestions, considering players' preferences, gameplay styles, genre inclinations, in-game choices, and past feedback to recommend game titles aligned with their interests. Adaptive difficulty, a gaming system, employs real-time player behavior analysis to customize game challenges. It evaluates factors like skill, response time, strategy, and progress speed to create personalized difficulty levels.

• *Book Publishing:* Authors send their work to publishers or literary agents in the manuscript submission and evaluation process. Editors and agents meticulously assess manuscripts, considering factors like quality, market potential, and alignment with the publisher's existing catalog. AI plays a pivotal role in the manuscript submission and evaluation process. AI also assists in efficient manuscript tracking, organized feedback management, and streamlining decision-making processes, ultimately enhancing the overall efficiency and effectiveness of the evaluation and publication process. In the critical editing and proofreading phase of manuscript preparation, AI proves to be a valuable tool. AI-driven grammar and spell-checking tools swiftly identify and rectify typographical and grammatical errors, ensuring an error-free manuscript. AI aids in graphic designs by providing design software with advanced features, like automated font suggestions based on genre, layout templates, and even predictive analytics to optimize design choices.

2.7 BENEFITS

The integration of AI in the media and entertainment industry has enabled companies to enhance services, personalize content, optimize operations, and engage audiences. By leveraging AI, the media and entertainment industry can now achieve unprecedented levels of efficiency and creativity. Leveraging AI-driven insights, media and entertainment companies gain a profound understanding of their audiences. They can anticipate preferences, curating captivating content that genuinely resonates with their desires. Other benefits of AI in media and entertainment industry include the following [10,16,17]:

• *Automation:* AI algorithms excel at automating repetitive tasks and suggesting productivity enhancements, allowing artists to focus on the more creative aspects of their work. In live broadcasting, AI automation will take center stage. It effortlessly handles real-time tasks such as closed captioning and provides dynamic graphics and informative overlays for sports events, news programs, and live shows. This can enhance the quality and accessibility of live content. Media companies are using AI-driven applications with natural language processing (NLP) capabilities to automate the process of adding captions or subtitles to television and film video assets. As AI continues to advance, the automation of post-production processes will further revolutionize how content is created. The automation of content creation and curation reduces production costs, making it more cost-effective for businesses.

• *Reduction of Human Error:* AI-driven automation minimizes the risk of mistakes that can occur during manual editing, ensuring more accurate results in processes like color correction, facial recognition, and compositing.

• *Lower Costs:* AI for media and entertainment is used to cut costs so that there is no necessity to hire numerous costly specialists to tackle specific tasks, further liberating the budget. AI aids businesses in media and entertainment by cutting costs through task automation. This diminishes labor expenses by reducing the reliance on human work, while AI-driven optimization concurrently curtails energy consumption, thereby lowering utility costs.

• *Improved Decision-making:* AI enhances business decision-making by analyzing extensive data for valuable insights. AI solutions development for media and entertainment typically involves creating systems that enhance decision-making, automate routine tasks, and personalize audience experiences. When companies comprehend their audience preferences, artificial intelligence in media helps produce content tailored toward a specific audience. An AI consulting company plays a pivotal role in assisting media companies to make strategic decisions regarding the type of entertainment worth investing in. AI algorithms can rapidly analyze vast volumes of data sourced from various channels, including social media engagement and viewing metrics, to discern consumer preferences.

• *Enhanced Accessibility:* AI-powered technologies such as speech recognition and natural language processing (NLP) enhance the accessibility of individuals with disabilities. Subtitles, closed captions and audio descriptions generated by AI algorithms make video content more accessible to viewers with hearing or vision impairments.

• *Personalization:* With the help of AI and machine learning, entertainment companies can analyze vast amounts of data to create personalized content recommendations, targeted advertising, and more. AI algorithms can analyze user data to offer personalized recommendations for movies, TV shows, and music. This helps entertainment companies to retain customers and improve their engagement with their content. As AI technology continues to improve, we expect more companies to adopt personalized strategies to engage consumers and increase revenue.

• *Production Efficiency:* AI can help improve the efficiency of production processes in the entertainment industry. For example, AI can automate video editing, voiceover, and post-production tasks, reducing the time and resources required. The gains in production efficiency will allow creatives to focus less on administrative and procedural tasks, which in turn will allow them to spend more time being creative.

• *Combatting Piracy:* Artificial Intelligence in media plays a crucial role in detecting and preventing copyright infringement and protecting intellectual property rights. AI-driven media solutions can identify and track pirated content across various platforms. AI in media and entertainment industry is helping to protect the creative works of artists and creators.

• *Audience Analysis:* AI can analyze audience behavior and feedback to provide insights on improving content and increasing engagement. This information can be used to create better content that resonates with audiences and improves the overall user experience.

• *Scalability:* As user-generated content grows exponentially, AI-based moderation tools provide the scalability needed to efficiently manage and moderate content across millions of posts and uploads, significantly reducing the need for manual oversight.

• *Monitoring Audience:* AI is capable of analyzing audience behavior and feedback to offer suggestions on how to improve content and boost engagement. With the use of this data, content creators may produce more engaging material that enhances user experience in general.

• *Marketing and Promotion:* To engage the target audience for a work, publishers and authors use marketing techniques. AI can create focused marketing and promotion plans by analyzing user data and social media trends. This enhances the marketing ROI for entertainment firms by assisting to target the relevant people.

Some of these benefits are displayed in Figure 2.8 [16].

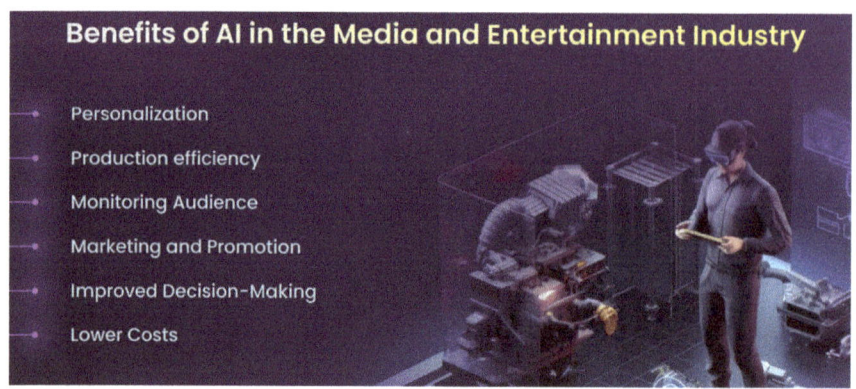

Figure 2.8 Some benefits of AI in media and entertainment [16].

2.8 CHALLENGES

Adopting AI technologies in the media and entertainment industries presents its own set of hurdles. Challenges such as quality control, copyright issues, job displacement, and ethical concerns with deepfake videos must be addressed. Staying attuned to emerging trends, learning, responding swiftly, and leveraging tailored AI-powered services are crucial. Enterprises often face challenges such as maintaining consistency, generating innovative ideas, ensuring originality, and meeting tight deadlines. Other challenges of AI in media and entertainment industry include the following [1,17]:

• *Degradation:* AI use in the media and entertainment industry risks becoming obsolete if human data scientists do not continuously train and assess it. The model and training data utilized to develop the AI will inevitably become outdated, making the AI obsolete unless it is retrained or programmed to learn and enhance itself autonomously.

• *Lack of Creativity:* While generative AI has the potential to expedite the creative process, there are numerous apprehensions surrounding the content it produces. Machines often lack the passion, nuance, and perspective in human-created works. Images generated by non-human entities, such as AI algorithms, lack the necessary human creative input and originality to qualify for intellectual property protection.

- *Quality Control:* Streaming speed and quality are crucial to engaged and content customers. AI The widespread use of AI, as demonstrated by the popularity of ChatGPT, has sparked concerns regarding the potential spread of disinformation. As AI-powered systems become more capable of generating news articles and other content, there is a growing concern that the reliability and authenticity of such AI-generated content may be compromised. Implementing robust fact-checking processes and integrating quality control mechanisms can help mitigate the risks associated with misinformation. The key lies in consistently delivering high-quality content that meets or exceeds the expectations of the audience.

- *Copyright:* Publishers frequently impose limitations on the usage of their content for AI learning processes. This is done to safeguard their intellectual property rights and prevent unauthorized use or replication of their work. However, such restrictions can sometimes lead to legal disputes between publishers and AI software manufacturers or developers who seek access to copyrighted materials for training AI models.

- *Job Loss:* The impact of AI on jobs is a major concern for professionals everywhere. With so many tasks being automated, the role of human experts is fast evolving. There is concern about job disruption for actors, writers, artists and other creative participants in the face of AI advancement. The emergence of AI in creative fields raises concerns among professionals working in those domains, such as art, photography, and copy editing. Professionals in these fields are grappling with the implications of AI's capabilities and the extent to which it may impact their roles and responsibilities. AI will result in fewer job opportunities for humans. Interestingly, younger generations perceive AI as creating opportunities, while older generations express pessimism and worry about potential skill replacement.

- *Ethical Concerns:* The use of AI in entertainment stirs up various controversies and ethical debates. Ethical concerns surrounding data privacy, intellectual property, and regulatory compliance continue to grow. The ethical dilemma arises from the potential harm caused by deepfake videos, as they can spread false information and have detrimental consequences. To mitigate the risk of unintended harm, when utilizing AI for content creation media and entertainment firms must ensure responsible and ethical practices. Gaining public acceptance of AI in the media and entertainment industry is of paramount importance.

• *Risks:* There were several warnings about three risks. First is the possibility of biased AI output due to biased or incomplete inputs. Second, misinformation can spread if there isn't full transparency on what content is AI-generated or on the provenance of the training data. Third, intellectual property issues are emerging from the use of generative AI to create or assist in the creation of text, audio, and video. Deepfake technology and synthetic media also introduce serious data protection risks.

• *Collaboration:* When teams operate independently, it creates communication gaps that can lead to disorder. In contrast, when teams collaborate, they tend to be more efficient. An essential strategy is collaboration between entertainment companies, AI developers, and regulatory bodies.

2.9 CONCLUSION

AI is undeniably transforming the media and entertainment industry, offering groundbreaking advancements in content creation, audience engagement, and personalization. AI in entertainment holds immense potential to revolutionize the industry and provide audiences with unprecedented engagement and enjoyment. AI offers a strategic advantage that is changing how content creators and exhibitors monetize their assets.

Integrating AI and data science has become powerful allies for media and entertainment firms. AI-powered tools are making storytelling, advertising, and digital content creation accessible to everyday users, shifting content production from professionals to a wider public audience. The media and entertainment companies are competitively working to develop AI technologies to pursue a worldwide audience. The goal is to provide billions of uniquely personalized user experiences, effectively creating an "audience of one" experience for every individual. As AI continues to reshape entertainment, industry leaders, regulators, and creators must adopt strategies that foster technological innovation while ensuring ethical safeguards and intellectual property (IP) protection [18]. More information on artificial intelligence in the M&E industry is available from the books in [19-23] and the following related journals:

- *The AI Journal*
- *AI Magazine*
- *Energy and AI*
- *Journal of Intelligence*

REFERENCES

[1] N. Sahota, "The transformative impact of AI on media and entertainment sectors," June 2023,

https://www.neilsahota.com/the-transformative-impact-of-ai-on-media-and-entertainment-sectors/

[2] H. Pokar, "Top benefits of implementing ai in the entertainment industry," March 2024,

https://www.bigscal.com/blogs/entertainment-industry/top-benefits-implementing-ai-entertainment-industry/

[3] M. N. O. Sadiku, S. A. Ajayi, and J. O. Sadiku, "Artificial intelligence in media and entertainment," *International Journal of Scientific and Academic Research*, vol. 5, no. 5, August 2025, pp. 1-14.

[4] M. N. O. Sadiku, "Artificial intelligence," *IEEE Potentials*, May 1989, pp. 35-39.

[5] "Artificial intelligence (AI),"

https://www.law.cornell.edu/wex/artificial_intelligence_(ai)

[6] "Artificial intelligence tutorial,"

https://www.javatpoint.com/artificial-intelligence-tutorial

[7] D. Quinby, "Artificial intelligence and the future of travel," May 2017,

https://www.phocuswright.com/Travel-Research/Research-Updates/2017/Artificial-Intelligence-and-the-Future-of-Travel

[8] "Generative AI explainer," Unknown Source.

[9] M. N. O. Sadiku, P. A. Adekunte, and J. O. Sadiku, "Generative artificial intelligence," *International Journal of Trend in Scientific Research and Development*, vol. 8, no. 6, November-December 2024, pp. 561-570.

[10] L. Hertz, "AI in media and entertainment: Use cases, benefits and solution,"

https://www.leewayhertz.com/ai-in-media-and-entertainment/

[11] "The transformative impact of AI in media and entertainment industry,"

https://tezeract.ai/ai-in-media-and-entertainment/

[12] S. Gopalakrishnan, "AI in media and entertainment: The revolution," March 2025,

https://vlinkinfo.com/blog/ai-in-media-and-entertainment-industry/

[13] "The impact of AI on media and entertainment industry,"

https://intellicoworks.com/impact-of-ai-on-media-and-entertainment-industry/

[14] "Generative AI in media & entertainment,"

https://www.brilworks.com/use-case/generative-ai-in-media-and-entertainment/

[15] J. Matuszewska, "How is AI used in entertainment? Use cases, examples, and tools," January 2025,

https://www.miquido.com/blog/how-is-ai-used-in-entertainment/

[16] M. Patel, "How does AI impact in entertainment and media industry?" March 2024,

https://www.concettolabs.com/blog/ai-impact-the-entertainment-and-media-industry/

[17] D. Singh, "Understanding the role of ai in media and entertainment," February 2024,

https://www.debutinfotech.com/blog/ai-in-media-and-entertainment

[18] M. Ozturk, "AI in entertainment: Balancing innovation and data protection," February 2025,

https://trendsresearch.org/insight/ai-in-entertainment-balancing-innovation-and-data-protection/?srsltid=AfmBOoquwM5_cpoWl1nmeUtCZ8rZl92_YQhEZYdMh29V7lOdrICtLRFx

[19] M. N. O. Sadiku, S. M. Musa, and S. R. Nelatury, *Applications of Artificial Intelligence*. Sherida, NY: Gotham Books, 2022.

[20] A. Connock, *Media Management and Artificial Intelligence*. Routledge, 2022.

[21] N. Hunter, *Artificial Intelligence in Entertainment: Will AI Help Us or Hurt Us? (Artificial Intelligence: Friend or Foe?)*. Cheriton Children's Books, 2024.

[22] D. Sumner, *AI in Entertainment and Media (The Artificial Intelligence Revolution)*. Kindle Edition, 2023.

[23] B. Williams, *The AI Revolution in Entertainment: Unleashing the Power of Artificial Intelligence to Shape the Future of Media (AI Unplugged: Navigating the World of Artificial Intelligence)*. Kindle Edition, 2023.

CHAPTER 3
ROBOTICS IN
MEDIA AND ENTERTAINMENT

"People with integrity do what they say they are going to do. Others have excuses."

— Laura Schlessinger

3.1 INTRODUCTION

The robots are shaped and designed to look like humans and can also be programmed to perform complex tasks and movements. In the ever-evolving landscape of technology, robots are no longer confined to industrial settings. They have seamlessly integrated into our daily lives, offering a myriad of possibilities, including media and entertainment.

Robots are popping up in unexpected places. They are hoisting pop stars over our heads, dancing with pianos, making cameos in blockbuster movies, and creating spectacles of color and light in venues large and small. Put them on the entertainment stage and now you have a performer's best friend. When robots go behind the scenes to help automate stage production, or special-effects photography and videography for commercials and movies, the plot thickens. Because like great performers, robots will keep pushing their limits [1].

Robotic technologies are applied in many areas of media and entertainment. This field leverages advanced robotics to enhance and revolutionize various forms of entertainment, from movies and theme parks to video games and live performances. Precision, repeatability, flexibility, reliability – just a few of the reasons robots are a great fit for the stage and screen. As robot prices continue to drop and integration gets easier, we expect to see more robots in the entertainment industry. Robots and AI are transforming film and TV production by automating various aspects, from camera operation and lighting to editing and post-production. These technologies increase efficiency and allow creators to focus on the creative aspects of their projects, resulting in higher quality productions [2].

Robotics in media and entertainment involves the design, development, and application of robots to create engaging and interactive experiences. It is a dynamic and rapidly evolving field that combines engineering, creativity, and technology to create innovative and immersive experiences. The importance of robotics in entertainment lies in its ability to create immersive experiences, push the boundaries of what is possible, and provide new forms of interaction and engagement for audiences. The entertainment industry is witnessing a revolutionary convergence of technology and creativity through the incorporation of robots [3].

This chapter examines the role of robots in media and entertainment. It begins with explaining what a robot is. It covers media and entertainment robots and their various types. It provides some applications of robotics in the media and entertainment industry. It highlights the benefits and challenges of robots in media and entertainment. The last section concludes with comments.

3.2 WHAT IS A ROBOT?

The word "robot" was coined by Czechriter Karel Čapek in his play in 1920. Isaac Asimov coined the term "robotics" in 1942 and came up with three rules to guide the behavior of robots and later added the zeroth law [4]:

- Law 0: A robot may not injure humanity or through inaction, allow humanity to come to harm.

- Law 1: Robots must never harm human beings,

- Law 2: Robots must follow instructions from humans without violating rule 1,

- Law3: Robots must protect themselves without violating the other rules.

Robots are becoming increasingly prevalent in almost every industry, from healthcare to manufacturing. Figure 3.1 indicates that robotics is one of the branches of artificial intelligence.

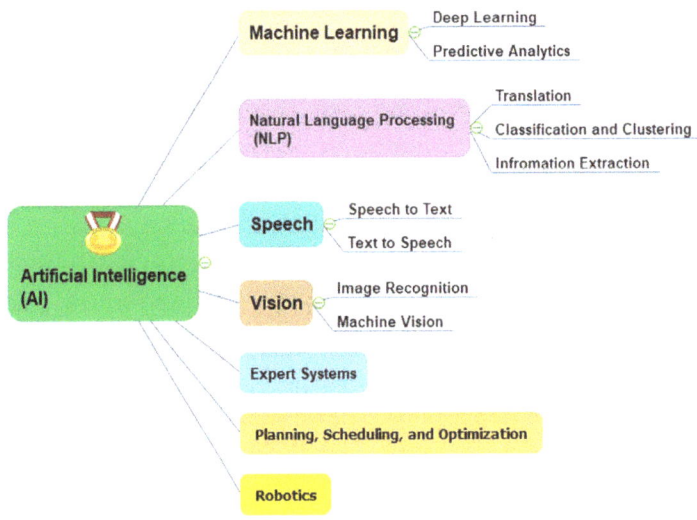

Figure 3.1 Robotics is one of the branches of artificial intelligence.

Although there are many types of robots designed for different environments and for different purposes/applications, they all share four basic similarities [5]:

(1) All robots have some form of mechanical construction designed to achieve a particular task;

(2) They have electrical components which power and control the machinery;

(3) All robots must be able to sense its surroundings; a robot may have light sensors (eyes), touch and pressure sensors (hands), chemical sensors (nose), hearing and sonar sensors (ears), etc.

(4) All robots contain some level of computer programming code.

Programs are the core essence of a robot since they provide intelligence. There are three different types of robotic programs: remote control, artificial intelligence, and hybrid. Some robots are programmed to faithfully carry out specific actions over and over again (repetitive actions) without variation and with a high degree of accuracy.

Robotics is an interdisciplinary field that involves the design, construction, operation, and use of robots. It is a branch of engineering and computer sciences that includes the design and use of machines that are capable of performing programmed tasks without human involvement. The field develops machines that can efficiently carry out various tasks, can automate tasks, and do various jobs that a human might not be able to do. Robots could someday be our drivers, companions, collaborators, teachers, specialists, and exploration pioneers [6].

3.3 MEDIA AND ENTERTAINMENT ROBOTS

Robotics in media and entertainment represents a fascinating intersection of technology, creativity, and engineering. An entertainment robot is a robot that is designed for the sole subjective pleasure of the human. It serves usually the owner or his housemates, guests, or clients. Entertainment robots can also be seen in the context of media arts where artists have been employing advanced technologies to create environments and artistic expression also utilizing actuators and sensors to allow their robots to react and change about viewers. The role of robotics in entertainment is growing at an exponential rate, pushing the boundaries of creativity and innovation. Whether in live performances, movies, theme parks, or interactive gaming, robots are revolutionizing how we experience entertainment. Figure 3.2 shows robots in media and entertainment [7].

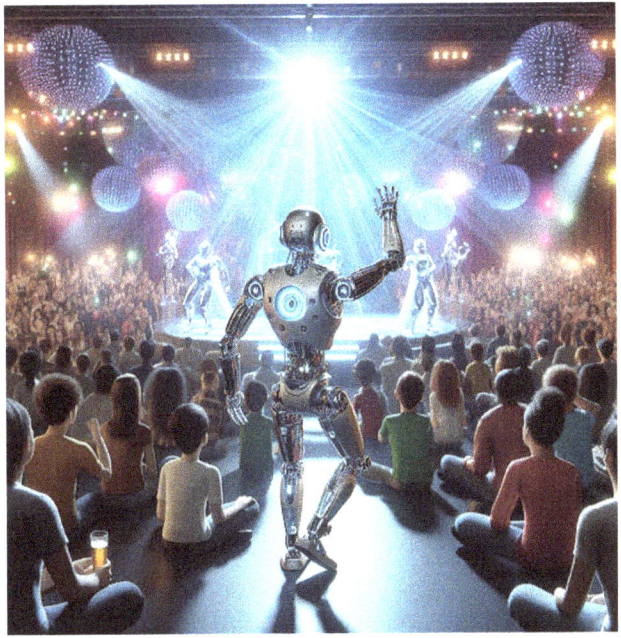

Figure 3.2 Robots in media and entertainment [7].

From the Middle Ages to the early 2020s, we trace the roots of entertainment robots. Robots have been serving as marketing devices for the best part of a thousand years. Robotics has been a growing staple across the entertainment industry for some time now. One of the most notable innovations in entertainment robotics is the advancement of robotics technology itself. From robots hosting live shows to autonomous production assistants, robotics is streamlining the entertainment production process. Companies have developed more agile, versatile, and interactive robots that can engage with audiences in a human-like manner. With AI capabilities, robots are becoming smarter, allowing for personalized interactions with users. Virtual reality and augmented reality are revolutionizing the entertainment industry, and their integration with robotics is taking immersive experiences to a whole new level [8]. For example, Sophia is the culmination of a series of robot projects undertaken by Hong Kong-based Hanson Robotics. Sophia is the first "artificial being" to address the United Nations and to be given citizenship of a country.

3.4 TYPES OF MEDIA AND ENTERTAINMENT ROBOTS

Most robots are designed for a single purpose that tends to exclusively define their form.

They are designed to appeal to us and to meet us on near-equal terms in our own physical space. Commercial media and entertainment robots include the following types [9]:

- *Collaborative Robot (Cobot):* A cobot is designed to work alongside humans, enhancing live performances and interactive exhibits.

- *Toy Robot:* Relatively cheap, mass-produced entertainment robots are used as mechanical, sometimes interactive, toys that perform various tasks and tricks on command. You do not have to visit a theatre to experience the wonders of modern robotics. Instead, you can have your personal source of robotic entertainment - with robotic toys or pets powered by artificial intelligence.

- *Robotic Dog:* Robot dogs as a fad have been produced with relatively little variation. For example, Teksta is a commercial toy robot dog popular in the 1990s. It was intended to be able to perform card tricks and respond to commands. Figure 3.3 shows an example of robotic dog [10].

Figure 3.3 A robotic dog [10].

- *Humanoid Robot:* Humanoid robots can interact with guests, provide information, and perform in shows. Despite those humanoid robots for utilitarian uses, some humanoid robots aim at entertainment uses, such as Sony's QRIO. They are usually capable of some advanced features like voice recognition or walking. The humanoid robots for entertainment is expanding with demand for lifelike, interactive experiences in theme parks, events, and media. An example of humanoid robot is shown in Figure 3.4 [11].

Figure 3.4 An example of humanoid robot [11].

- *Companion Robot:* Robots can serve as companions, providing entertainment and emotional.

3.5 APPLICATIONS OF ROBOTICS IN MEDIA AND ENTERTAINMENT

Robotics has a wide range of applications across various industries. It is increasingly used in the media and entertainment industry for a variety of applications, including film and television production, live events, theme parks, and even in the creation of new forms of art. Common applications include the following [7,12,13]:

- *Automation:* Robots can automate tasks, enhance creativity, and create immersive experiences for audiences. They are used to perform tasks autonomously or semi-autonomously, reducing the need for human intervention. Deloitte predicts that more than 40% of tasks in the media and entertainment industry could be automated by 2025. Improved automation could address industry challenges like rising production costs and fluctuating audience demand. Automation can streamline post-production tasks, such as video editing and special effects, freeing up human resources for more creative decision-making roles.

• *Film and Television:* Robots are used extensively in the film and television industry to create lifelike characters and special effects. Animatronics bring creatures and characters to life, while motion capture technology allows actors' movements to be translated into digital animations. Examples include the animatronic dinosaurs in "Jurassic Park" and the motion-captured characters in "Avatar." Robots can control cameras for complex shots and stabilize footage. Robotics can assist with stop-motion animation, making adjustments frame-by-frame. Drone filming has also started to enter the sphere with drone shows famously taking place in Dubai and at special events around the world. Figure 3.5 shows a typical drone [14].

Figure 3.5 A typical drone [14].

• *Theme Parks:* Theme parks are embracing robotics in entertainment to elevate visitor experiences and create attractions that were once deemed impossible. Robotic amusement park rides have also become a mainstay at funfairs and carnivals around the world to cater to visitors, as well as robot servers in restaurants and at exhibitions. Theme parks utilize robotics to create immersive and interactive experiences for visitors. Animatronic figures populate rides and attractions, providing lifelike interactions. For instance, Disney's "Pirates of the Caribbean" ride features highly detailed animatronic pirates, while Universal Studios' "Harry Potter and the Forbidden Journey" ride uses robotic arms to simulate flying on a broomstick. Robots can be integrated into rides and attractions, creating more engaging experiences. They can be used to create animatronic characters in theme parks and other venues.

• *Live Performances:* Robots are increasingly being used in live performances, such as concerts, theater productions, and art installations. Robots have started to make a significant impact in live entertainment, captivating audiences with their precision and futuristic appeal. Robotic dancers, musicians, and even actors are appearing in live shows, offering performances that blend human creativity with mechanical accuracy. Robotic systems can control lighting, sound, and stage effects, creating dynamic and engaging shows. For example, the band Muse has used drones and robotic lighting systems in their live performances to create a futuristic atmosphere. Robots can control lighting, camera angles, and sound systems, creating dynamic and immersive experiences.

• *Storytelling:* Robots equipped with artificial intelligence (AI) are transforming the storytelling landscape. These intelligent beings can dynamically adapt narratives based on audience reactions, creating a truly interactive experience. Whether it is a robot-led theater production or an AI-driven storytelling session for children, the possibilities are boundless. The fusion of technology and creativity opens doors to a new era of narrative entertainment.

• *Sports:* Sports enthusiasts are in for a treat as robots enter the arena, showcasing their prowess in physical competitions. From robot soccer tournaments to drone racing leagues, these events not only push the boundaries of technology but also provide a thrilling spectacle for fans. The precision and speed of robotic athletes add a futuristic charm to traditional sports, attracting a new generation of viewers. Figure 3.6 shows a robot for sports [15].

Figure 3.6 A robot for sports [15].

• *Robo-Comedians:* Laughter is a universal language, and robots are learning to speak it fluently. Robotic comedians are gaining popularity in entertainment circuits, delivering jokes with impeccable timing and a touch of mechanical humor. These comedic bots not only entertain but also challenge our perceptions of creativity and wit in artificial entities.

• *Gaming:* Gaming has evolved from pixels on a screen to immersive experiences, and robots are taking it a step further. Imagine a gaming session where physical robots become an integral part of the gameplay. From real-life robot battles to collaborative gaming experiences, the fusion of robotics and gaming is a testament to the limitless potential of entertainment technology. Robotics technology enhances video games through motion capture and VR/AR systems. Motion capture allows for realistic character animations, while VR and AR provide immersive gaming experiences.

• *Robot Journalism:* Robots are used to generate news articles, freeing up human journalists for more complex tasks.

• *Robotic Musicians:* Robots can play music, even compose their own music. AI-powered robotic bands, such as Compressorhead, are playing instruments with unmatched precision, creating a mesmerizing experience for audiences.

3.6 BENEFITS

Robots do not flinch in the face of danger. They can consistently repeat the same movement, ensuring that the risky shots are captured perfectly without endangering human lives. Robotics, with its blend of precision, consistency, and innovation, is undeniably playing a pivotal role in modern film production. Robots can attract larger crowds in entertainment settings, offer unique experiences that set a venue apart from competitors, and reduce labor costs by automating certain services. Other benefits of robotics in media and entertainment include the following [16]:

• *Interactivity:* Robots can be programmed to react to stimuli in their environment. This interactivity is particularly useful in scenes that require real-time feedback. For example, a robotic character could react to an actor's lines or movements, ensuring a dynamic and natural interaction between humans and machines.

• *Precision:* Stop-motion, one of the oldest film techniques, has been given a new life through robotics. Instead of manually adjusting models frame-by-frame, robots can be programmed to make the finest adjustments, resulting in smoother animations. Such precision reduces the margin of error and ensures a higher quality output.

• *Sustainability:* As sustainability becomes an increasingly important factor in consumer decision-making, robotics companies are focusing on creating eco-friendly robots. This includes using sustainable materials and energy-efficient designs, making entertainment robots more environmentally conscious. Robotics, especially when paired with renewable energy sources, can significantly reduce the carbon footprint of film production. Automated systems can manage resources more efficiently, while 3D printed sets often require fewer materials, resulting in less waste.

- *Collaboration:* These mechanical marvels are not merely tools but collaborators, pushing the boundaries of what is possible in the realms of performance, storytelling, sports, gaming, music, film, art, and live events. Collaboration between engineers, artists, and ethicists can help address technical and ethical challenges.

3.7 CHALLENGES

In spite of the exciting possibilities, there are several challenges and considerations associated with robotics in entertainment. The use of AI and data collection in entertainment raises concerns about user privacy and data security. Other challenges of robotics in media and entertainment include [12]:

- *Complexity:* Designing and developing advanced robotic systems is complex and requires expertise in multiple engineering disciplines.

- *Cost:* High costs associated with developing and maintaining robotic systems can be a barrier for some applications.

- *Reliability:* Ensuring the reliability and safety of robotic systems, especially in live performances, is critical.

- *Job Displacement:* The increasing use of robots in entertainment may lead to job displacement for certain roles.

- *Regulation:* Developing regulations and standards for the use of robotics in entertainment can ensure safety and ethical considerations are met. The regulatory landscape for humanoid robots in entertainment is still evolving, with key considerations around safety, privacy, and ethical use of AI. Compliance with existing and forthcoming regulations is crucial for companies to navigate to avoid potential legal challenges and to foster public trust in this technology.

- *Research and Development:* Continued research and development can lead to more cost-effective and reliable robotic systems.

3.8 CONCLUSION

As the field of robotics continues to evolve, the integration of robotics in entertainment is becoming increasingly sophisticated, offering endless possibilities for innovation and creativity. As robots continue to evolve and become more sophisticated, their role in entertainment is destined to expand. Anticipated advancements include more lifelike and interactive robotic performers, increased use of AI-driven storytelling, integration of robots in virtual and augmented reality experiences, and the development of AI-powered characters for theme parks and live events. Greater advances in artificial intelligence and robotics will lead to more applications of robotics in entertainment along with improvements in the existing applications [17]. More information on robotics in the media and entertainment industry can be found in the books in [18,19] and the following related journals:

- *Robotica*
- *Robotics*
- *Robitics and Autonomous*
- *Robotics and Computer-Integrated Manufacturing,*
- *Advanced Robotics*
- *Autonomous Robots*
- *Automation in Construction*
- *Journal of Robotics*
- *Journal of Robotic Systems*
- *Journal of Robotic Surgery*
- *Journal of Robotics and Mechatronics*
- *Journal of Intelligent & Robotic Systems*
- *Journal of Mechanisms and Robotics-Transactions of the ASME*
- *Journal of Automation, Mobile Robotics and Intelligent*

Systems

- *Journal of Future Robot Life*
- *IEEE Robotics and Automation Letters*
- *IEEE Transactions on Robotics*
- *International Journal of Robotics Research*
- *International Journal of Social Robotics*
- *International Journal of Humanoid Robotics*
- *International Journal of Advanced Robotic Systems*
- *Science Robotics*
- *Soft Robotics*

REFERENCES

[1] T. M. Anandan, "Elevating the art of entertainment – Robotically," July 2017,

https://www.automate.org/robotics/industry-insights/elevating-the-art-of-entertainment-robotically

[2] D. Russon, "Future focus friday: AI and robotics in the entertainment industry," July 2024,

https://www.linkedin.com/pulse/future-focus-friday-ai-robotics-entertainment-industry-dominic-russo-mqt7c/

[3] M. N. O. Sadiku, P. A. Adekunte, and J. O. Sadiku, "Robotics in media and entertainment," *International Journal of Trend in Scientific Research and Development*, vol. 9, no. 3, May-June 2025, pp. 483-490.

[4] "Human–robot interaction," *Wikipedia*, the free encyclopedia

https://en.wikipedia.org/wiki/Human–robot_interaction

[5] "Robotics," *Wikipedia*, the free encyclopedia

h6tps://en.wikipedia.org/wiki/Robotics

[6] M. N. O. Sadiku, U. C. Chukwu. A. Ajayi-Majebi, and S. M. Musa, "A primer on robotics," *International Journal of Trend in Scientific Research and Development*, vol. 6, no. 7, November-December 2022, pp. 614-621.

[7] G. Sarraf, "Robotics in entertainment: Transforming the future of media & fun," February 2025,

https://thinkrobotics.com/blogs/learn/robotics-in-entertainment-transforming-the-future-of-media-fun?srsltid=AfmBOoolLgUr85 0AsYrNlfbubK2bDEMAkwFww_Me8IIl_momZ29R1RpE

[8] "Entertainment robotics market technology shifts & growth challenges," April 2025,

https://www.linkcdin.com/pulse/entertainment-robotics-market-technology-shifts-growth-challenges-2nbgf/

[9] "Entertainment robot," *Wikipedia*, the free encyclopedia

https://en.wikipedia.org/wiki/Entertainment_robot

[10] S. Evans, "Boston Dynamics' spot: The design behind the robot dog," November 2022,

https://www.iotworldtoday.com/robotics/boston-dynamics-spot-the-design-behind-the-robot-dog

[11] J. Biba, "Top 27 humanoid robots in use right now,"

https://builtin.com/robotics/humanoid-robots

[12] "Robotics in entertainment,

https://www.discoverengineering.org/robotics-in-entertainment/

[13] "How can robots be used for entertainment? 10 creative ways," December 2023,

https://provenrobotics.ai/how-can-robots-be-used-for-entertainment/

[14] J. Wilson, "How robotics in the entertainment industry could intertwine with other sectors for growth," June 2022,

https://www.forbes.com/sites/joshwilson/2022/06/06/how-robotics-in-the-entertainment-industry-could-intertwine-with-other-sectors-for-growth/

[15] "When robots take the field: Will AI ruin sports?"

https://www.oxford-aiethics.ox.ac.uk/blog/when-robots-take-field-will-ai-ruin-sports

[16] L. Tyron, "How robotics is revolutionizing film production," August 2023,

https://medium.com/@leontyron/how-robotics-is-revolutionizing-film-production-eeb5e79cccd5

[17] T. Austin-Morgan, "Lessons learned by roboticists in the entertainment industry are filtering back into industry," January

2019,

https://www.allerin.com/blog/robotics-is-taking-over-the-entertainment-industry

[18] M. N. O. Sadiku, *Robotics and Its Applications*. Moldova, Europe: Lambert Academic Publishing, 2023.

[19] M. Soni, *Robotics: Text Book*. Ebook, 2024.

CHAPTER 4
DRONES IN
MEDIA AND ENTERTAINMENT

"My whole thing is to entertain, make people laugh and to forget about the real world for a while."

— Dan Aykroyd

4.1 INTRODUCTION

The media and entertainment (M&E) industry encompasses a diverse range of businesses involved in the creation, production, distribution, and monetization of content across various platforms. This includes film, television, music, gaming, sports, publishing, and digital media. With rapid technological advancements and shifting consumer preferences, the industry continually evolves, presenting both challenges and opportunities for professionals engaged in content creation, distribution, and digital transformation strategies [1]. One innovative tool that has revolutionized the industry is drone technology. High demand for drones has recently developed in a slightly unexpected market, the entertainment industry, where the purpose of drones is to enhance performance.

Drones offer a unique perspective and versatility that traditional filming methods cannot match. They have become a game-changer in various industries. These flying marvels have made a significant impact on the entertainment industry, particularly in ways that might surprise you. Major live events such as concerts and sports broadcasting have embraced the use of drones to enhance the visual effects for the audience. Drones provide a unique perspective that captures the energy and excitement of these events in a way that was not possible before. They bring a new dimension to the viewing experience by offering dynamic shots that traditional cameras cannot achieve. We have since witnessed drones playing increasingly vital roles in the production of many of Hollywood's biggest film blockbusters [2]. Figure 4.1 shows a typical use of drones [3].

Figure 4.1 A typical use of drones [3].

Drones are bringing about radical change in the worlds of agriculture, inspection, real estate, and beyond. They have revolutionized the media and entertainment industry, offering new perspectives, increased efficiency, and innovative storytelling possibilities. They have brought new creative ways, given cheaper choices, improved safety and ease of access, and made the overall quality of movies and media projects better. The advent of drone cinematography has revolutionized filmmaking and video production, opening up new creative possibilities. Drones are taking unmanned aerial photography services to new heights, making it an accessible hobby that anyone can get started in [4].

In this chapter, we will explore the role of drones in the media and entertainment industry. The chapter begins with explaining what a drone is. It describes drones in the media and entertainment industry and provides some of their applications. It highlights the benefits and challenges of drones in media and entertainment. The last section conclude with comments.

4.2 WHAT IS A DRONE?

At least three terms are used to describe drones, depending on how they are operated. The terms include Unmanned Aerial Vehicles (UAVs), Unpiloted Aircraft System (UAS), and Remote Piloted Aircraft System (RPAS). The FAA defines drones, also known as unmanned aerial vehicles (UAVs), as any aircraft system without a flight crew onboard. Drones include flying, floating, and other devices, including unmanned aerial vehicles (UAVs), that can fly independently along set routes using an onboard computer or follow commands transmitted remotely by a pilot on the ground. A typical drone is shown in Figure 4.2 [5]. A drone is usually controlled remotely by a human pilot on the ground, as typically shown in Figure 4.3 [5].

Figure 4.2 A typical drone [5].

Figure 4.3 A drone is usually controlled by operators on the ground [5].

Drones can range in size from large military drones to smaller drones. Drones, previously used for military purposes, have started to be used for civilian purposes since the 2000s. Since then, drones have continued to be used in intelligence, aerial surveillance, search and rescue, reconnaissance, and offensive missions as part of the military Internet of things (IoT). Today, drones are used for different purposes such as aerial photography, surveillance, agriculture, entertainment, healthcare, transportation, law enforcement, etc.

Drones work much like other modes of air transportation, such as helicopters and airplanes. When the engine is turned on, it starts up, and the propellers rotate to enable flight. The motors spin the propellers and the propellers push against the air molecules downward, which pulls the drone upwards. Once the drone is flying, it is able to move forward, back, left, and right by spinning each of the propellers at a different speed. Then, the pilot uses the remote control to direct its flight from the ground [6],

Drone laws exist to ensure a high level of safety in the skies, especially near sensitive areas like airports. They also aim to address privacy concerns that arise when camera drones fly in residential areas. These include the requirement to keep your drone within sight at all times when airborne. In the United States, drones weighing less than 250g are exempt from registration with civil aviation authorities. If your drone exceeds 250g in weight, you will also require a Flyer ID, which requires passing a test [7]. It is necessary to register as an operator, be trained as a pilot, and have civil liability insurance, in addition to complying with various flight regulations, and those of the places where their use is permitted.

Most drones have a limited payload, usually under 11 pounds. Drones are classified according to their size. Here are the different drone types:

- Nano Drone: 80-100 mm

- Micro Drone: 100-150 mm

- Small Drone: 150-250 mm

- Medium Drone: 250-400 mm

- Large Drone: 400+ mm

One of the emerging trends in drone use for factories is the utilization of LiDAR technology. LiDAR stands for Light Detection and Ranging. This technology provides accurate depth information essential for understanding the three-dimensional structure of the environment. LiDAR sensors emit laser beams to measure distances to objects, creating high-resolution 3D maps of the surrounding terrain and objects. The ability to capture detailed data through LiDAR technology has opened up opportunities for better predictive maintenance, reduction in inspection times, and overall cost savings [8].

4.3 DRONES IN MEDIA AND ENTERTAINMENT

Drones are no longer confined to construction sites or technical projects. They have evolved into essential tools for filmmakers, event organizers, and even theme parks. These unmanned aerial vehicles (UAVs) are opening new creative possibilities in entertainment. They have revolutionized the entertainment industry, changing the rules of the game as we knew it. Their ability to fly with precision, and capture images from impossible perspectives has transformed the way certain events and audiovisual productions can be enjoyed.

The origins of drones can be traced back to World War I. For many decades since then, drones have been extensively used for military purposes. Drones were initially developed as military tools for surveillance and targeted air strikes. That history makes many people around the world uncomfortable with their use in civilian settings. The US military first began developing and flying unmanned drones in Afghanistan in 2000. In recent years, however, drones have also become increasingly popular in the entertainment industry. Drone technology is changing the way movie makers operate, and it is literally changing how Hollywood, the Mecca of movie-making, produces films for public consumption. Drones have become a hot commodity now, after finally hitting the market and becoming accessible for the average consumer to purchase [9].

4.4 APPLICATIONS OF DRONES IN MEDIA AND ENTERTAINMENT

Drones are used in filmmaking, advertising, news coverage, and live events, enhancing visual experiences and capturing content that would be difficult or impossible with traditional methods. Common areas of application of drones in the M&E industry include the following [10-12]:

• *Aerial Photography and Cinematography:* Photography and cinematography have reached great new heights thanks to drone technology. Perhaps more than any other technological development of the past decade or two, the aerial photography provided by drone technology is having a massive impact on the way movies are made. Drones can go places that no other devices can, and in ways that even the most sophisticated photography equipment simply cannot match. The only thing even close to that would have been a helicopter shot, and helicopters are so big and bulky that they simply cannot get into all the places that drones can, nor can they fly as low. Aerial cinematography involves the skill of capturing video or film footage from an elevated position using specialized equipment like helicopters, balloons, or other aerial platforms, which may include drones. Equipped with advanced cameras and stabilized gimbal systems, these drones enable filmmakers to achieve cinematic shots from unique perspectives that were previously inaccessible or prohibitively expensive. This technology has revolutionized cinematography by offering versatile tools for creating visually stunning sequences and enhancing storytelling with dynamic aerial perspectives. A typical drone used for aerial photography is shown in Figure 4.4 [13].

Figure 4.4 A typical drone used for aerial photography [13].

• *Film and Television:* The film and TV industry has changed much because of drone technology. Using drones has become very important in making films and TV today because of the new creative chances they bring. Since the establishment of the film industry, storytellers, screenwriters, and producers have always looked for ways to make movies all the more enjoyable. Filmmakers are increasingly relying on drones to capture shots that would be difficult or dangerous with traditional cameras. Before drones, achieving dramatic aerial views often required expensive helicopter rentals and extensive safety measures. Drones have changed the game by making it easier, safer, and more affordable to capture breathtaking aerial footage. Drones allow filmmakers to capture stunning aerial shots, dynamic angles, and fluid camera movements, creating more immersive and visually impactful scenes. They enable filmmakers to access tight spaces or tricky environments where traditional cameras cannot go. An example of film production using drones is shown in Figure 4.5 [2].

Figure 4.5 An example of film production using drones [2].

• *Live Shows:* When you think of live entertainment, you might imagine traditional elements like lights, pyrotechnics, or dancers. However, drones are now being used as actual performers, choreographed to move in sync and create mesmerising visual spectacles. Drone light shows, in particular, are taking the entertainment world by storm. They are often used during major events, such as sports games, music festivals, New Year's Eve celebrations or corporate celebrations, adding a new level of excitement. Drones equipped with LED lights create mesmerizing aerial displays and light shows, enhancing live performances and creating unforgettable experiences. One of the most impressive developments in the world of entertainment is the use of drones to create light shows. An example is the spectacle during the Tokyo 2020 Olympic Games, where more than 1,800 drones formed a dazzling floating globe VIDEO. Figure 4.6 shows an example of light show using drones [14].

Figure 4.6 An example of light show using drones [14].

• *Live Broadcasts:* Live broadcasts have reached new heights thanks to drones. Whether it is covering sports events, concerts, or even award shows, drones are revolutionizing how audiences experience live entertainment. For example, in sports like surfing, skiing, or motorsports, drones can follow athletes in real-time, offering an up-close and personal view of the action without being intrusive. Broadcasters are now able to bring the audience right into the heart of the action, capturing the intensity of a game or race from never-before-seen angles.

• *Sports Broadcasting:* Sports broadcasting has been revolutionized by the integration of drones, offering a dynamic perspective that enhances the viewing experience. In outdoor recreation events such as marathons and cycling races, drones provide stunning aerial shots that capture the essence of the competition. Drones are now a staple in advertising campaigns for sports events, enabling brands to reach a vast audience through captivating aerial footage. The ability to deliver real-time action from unique vantage points adds a new dimension to sports coverage, engaging audiences in ways previously unattainable.

• *Theme Parks:* Beyond live performances, drones are being used in virtual reality (VR) experiences within theme parks. Drones are increasingly becoming a staple in the magical world of theme parks. Behind the scenes, skilled drone pilots work tirelessly to capture breathtaking aerial shots that seamlessly blend into the park's multimedia content. Theme parks have always been about creating immersive experiences, and drones are now playing a vital role in enhancing that magic. Some theme parks are incorporating drones into their live-action stunt shows, using them to simulate flying objects, spaceships, or magical creatures. These drones are carefully synchronized with other effects, like sound and lighting, to create realistic and thrilling moments for park visitors. From creating mesmerizing music videos to capturing behind-the-scenes footage for virtual reality experiences, the versatility of drones in theme parks is truly remarkable.

• *Music Videos:* Music videos have evolved significantly over the years, incorporating cutting-edge technology to enhance their visual appeal. With the advent of drones in photography, artists are now able to capture stunning aerial shots that were once only possible with expensive helicopters or cranes. Incorporating drones into music videos also allows for the creation of cinematic shots that rival those seen in blockbuster films. The ability to soar above cityscapes or natural landscapes adds a sense of grandeur and scale to the videos, immersing viewers in a virtual reality experience that feels both intimate and expansive. The dynamic movements and sweeping panoramas captured by drones add a sense of drama and excitement to the visuals, elevating the overall production value of the video.

• *Advertising:* Drones have emerged as powerful instruments for advertisers and marketers. Film and advertising have not been left behind in the adoption of drones. Their ability to capture images from previously impossible heights and angles has allowed filmmakers to create stunning, dynamic shots without the need for expensive helicopters or cranes. In advertising, drones are used for creative on-location shoots, capturing footage in an innovative and aesthetically appealing way. These advances have not only reduced production costs but have opened up new storytelling possibilities for content creators.

• *Journalism:* In the United States, the unfiltered information that journalists provide to the public serves as an important check on the country's three branches of government: executive, legislative, and judicial. Journalism has rapidly evolved over the years thanks to advancements in technology that have produced new tools and techniques for news gathering and dissemination. To date, data journalism and artificial intelligence have taken center stage in discussions on the impact of technology on journalism. Drones have proven to be powerful investigative journalism tools. Drone journalism, which is the use of drones or unmanned aerial vehicles for news gathering, is on the rise across the African continent. Drone journalism provides a safer and more cost-effective way for journalists to capture footage in dangerous or remote locations. Drones can be used to monitor natural disasters, capture footage of conflict zones, and report on other events that require aerial coverage. Drone technology allows journalists to take footage of news events such as volcanic eruptions, war-torn villages, and natural disasters. Drones can be useful tools for obtaining aerial images and news footage of areas that would otherwise be difficult to cover, such as those struck by natural disasters and conflict zones. Figure 4.7 show a quadcopter drone with a camera for new coverage [15].

Figure 4.7 A quadcopter drone with a camera for new coverage [15].

• *Tourism and Hospitality:* Drones have become a staple in travel and hospitality marketing, playing a crucial role in enticing travelers with visually appealing content. They capture stunning aerial shots of destinations, resorts, and attractions, offering potential tourists a sneak peek into the experiences that await them. These captivating visuals inspire travelers to plan their trips and explore the world.

4.5 BENEFITS

Drones bring a new dimension to the viewing experience by offering dynamic shots that traditional cameras cannot achieve. They improve safety by reducing the need for human presence in hazardous filming locations. They offer flexibility and accessibility, allowing for filming in hard-to-reach places. With advancements in drone technology, live event organizers can now create stunning aerial shots that add a dynamic element to the overall experience for viewers. One of the primary benefits of incorporating drones into film production is the cost-effectiveness they offer compared to traditional aerial cinematography methods. Other benefits of drones in media and entertainment include the following [16-18]:

• *Cost Savings:* The low cost of using drones is a major benefit that makes them liked in the film and media industry. Instead of having to rent out expensive cranes or pay for high-cost helicopter rentals, a production crew can now use a relatively low-cost drone to capture a higher-quality shot on film and save a ton of money in the process. The cost for renting a very capable drone might only be 25% of the cost of renting other more expensive equipment, and the resulting film would not be as good.

• *Time Savings:* In another big savings bonanza, the time needed to set up a shot with drones is considerably less than it would be with any other type of equipment, which is a godsend to independent filmmakers with limited resources. Scenes that used to require 5 to 10 cameras and an entire filming crew, can now be captured with less than 30 minutes of setup time, and only three crew members to pull it off.

• *Enhanced Aerial Perspectives:* Incorporating drones into corporate video production offers a revolutionary way to capture stunning aerial shots. Unlike traditional filming methods that rely on cranes or helicopters, drones can effortlessly glide through the air, providing unparalleled access to various altitudes and angles. This flexibility allows for the creation of dynamic and engaging visuals that were previously difficult or impossible to achieve.

• *Real-Time Monitoring:* Another important benefit of using drones in making films and media is that they can show video while recording. Drones have live feeds so directors and camera operators can watch what the drone sees instantly. This helps them to change the shots immediately as needed. This real-time watching makes sure the right angles and compositions are achieved, lessening the need for reshooting and saving important production time.

• *Flexibility and Accessibility:* One of the most significant advantages of using drones in corporate video production is their remarkable flexibility. Drones can effortlessly navigate various environments, from urban landscapes to rugged terrains, enabling filmmakers to capture footage from virtually any location. Unlike traditional camera setups that are often limited by ground-based constraints, drones can soar above obstacles and provide unique perspectives that enhance the visual appeal of corporate videos.

• *Engaging Storytelling:* Drones have revolutionized corporate video production by adding dynamic elements that were previously hard to achieve. Their ability to capture smooth, sweeping shots from various angles introduces a new level of cinematic quality to corporate videos. This dynamic range of motion helps in creating more engaging and visually appealing content.

• *Advertising:* Drones offer a unique perspective for showcasing products and locations, making ads more engaging and visually appealing. Drones in the cinema and advertising industry have not been left behind in the adoption of drones.

• *Drone Pilot:* The secret to succeeding as a drone pilot for film and video production stems from one thing: a passion for aviation, technology, and photography. Becoming a drone pilot is the perfect way to combine all of these interests. Pilots must acquire numerous flight hours, advanced operating and flying skills, familiarity with given equipment and obtain relevant FAA certifications.

• *Ubiquitous Utilization:* As with any new technology, it has taken a little while for drone usage to catch on, but now that it has; it is seemingly everywhere, both in television and in movie scenes. Because the potential applications for drone videography is virtually limitless, more and more studios are becoming aware of the benefits, and are incorporating them as part of the production process.

4.6 CHALLENGES

While drones have opened up new creative possibilities in filmmaking and video production, they also present a unique set of challenges and limitations that must be addressed. Although drones are a relatively cost-effective method of obtaining aerial footage, they can still be prohibitively expensive for smaller newsrooms, particularly the high cost of training journalists on how to use them safely. As drones continue to shape the entertainment industry, the demand for skilled pilots is on the rise. Other challenges of drones in media and entertainment include the following [19,20]:

• *Privacy:* Privacy is a fundamental human right and its protection is crucial to the preservation of other rights, like freedom of expression and the right to personal security. Despite the risk of these regulations being weaponized against journalists, there are key questions around the need to protect privacy when promoting the use of drones. Although there might be legitimate newsgathering interests, citizens do have a reasonable expectation of privacy. There are concerns that, in the absence of adequate legal protections, drones could be used to surveil citizens.

• *Safety:* Drones can be dangerous. There have been a rash of incidents, mostly involving drones operated by hobbyists. It is crucial for filmmakers and video production teams to prioritize legal and safety considerations. Safety concerns are paramount when operating drones on film sets or during live-streaming events. These unmanned aerial vehicles can pose risks to crew members, actors, and bystanders if not operated properly. Comprehensive safety protocols, risk assessments, and experienced pilots are crucial to mitigating potential hazards and ensuring a safe working environment. Filmmakers must ensure that their drone pilots are properly certified and trained to operate drones safely and legally, mitigating potential risks.

• *Ethics:* Journalism ethics require that a balance be struck between the right to privacy and journalists' duty to inform the public. Provision to laws regulating drone use would help strike the necessary balance between safeguarding citizens' privacy and allowing journalists to pursue their investigations freely. This potentially prevents journalists from reporting on public interest stories that take place on private property. Journalists should be trained to use drones safely and to apply ethical standards.

• *Regulations:* Legal restrictions and regulations play a vital role in the use of drones for film production and content creation. Regulation can also be used to shut down access to this technology entirely. In many countries and jurisdictions, there are strict rules governing where drones can fly. In Kenya, for example, civilian drone use was banned between March 2019 and November 2020, due to privacy concerns. Now that the ban has been lifted, drone use remains impeded by a lengthy and expensive registration process, which can cost thousands of dollars. Similarly, in Nigeria, drone licensing costs can be prohibitively expensive for smaller newsrooms.

• *Weather:* One of the most significant challenges is the impact of weather conditions. Drones are sensitive to wind, rain, and other environmental factors, which can impact their flight performance and the quality of the drone footage captured. Pilots must thoroughly inspect their equipment, assess weather conditions, and identify potential hazards or obstacles in the filming location.

• *Battery Life:* Battery life is another crucial consideration in drone cinematography. Most professional-grade drones have a limited flight time of around 20-30 minutes, which can be a constraint for certain shooting scenarios or extended takes. Careful planning, efficient battery management, and the use of backup power sources are essential to ensure smooth and uninterrupted aerial filming operations.

• *Technical Limitations:* Drones have limitations, especially when it comes to filming high-speed action scenes. Technical limitations, such as range and interference, can impact the effectiveness of drone cinematography. Certain environments or locations may have signal interference or obstructions that can disrupt the drone's performance, communication with the pilot, or the quality of the captured footage. Furthermore, drones have limitations in their payload capacity and the types of cameras and equipment they can carry.

4.7 CONCLUSION

Filmmakers now have a powerful tool at their disposal to capture stunning visuals from unique and dynamic perspectives. By incorporating drone shots into their projects, filmmakers can enhance the overall production value of their films, immersing viewers in breathtaking aerial vistas that elevate the storytelling experience. Major live events such as concerts and sports broadcasting have embraced the use of drones to enhance the visual effects for the audience. As drone technology keeps getting better, we can look forward to more creative and amazing uses of drones in film and media.

With advancements in drone technology, live event organizers can now create stunning aerial shots that add a dynamic element to the overall experience for viewers. Only time will tell how drones will continue to change media and entertainment as we know it. The future of drone cinematography holds exciting possibilities as technology continues to evolve and push boundaries. Advancements in camera technology, such as higher resolution sensors, improved dynamic range, and better low-light performance, will further enhance the quality of drone footage. More information about drones in the media and entertainment industry can be found in the books in [21-24].

REFERENCES

[1] "Applications of GPS drone in the media and entertainment industry,"

https://gaotek.com/applications-of-gps-drone-in-media-and-entertainment-industry/

[2] P. Ip, "Drones in Hollywood: How Have Drones Changed the Film & Movie Industry," July 2022,

https://www.adorama.com/alc/drones-hollywood-film-movie-industry/

[3] "The revolutionary role of drones in the film and entertainment industry,"

https://whitehawkmedia.com/the-revolutionary-role-of-drones-in-the-film-and-entertainment-industry/

[4] M. N. O. Sadiku, P. O. Adebo, and J. O. Sadiku, "Drones in entertainment," *International Journal of Trend in Research and Development*, vol. 11, no. 5, September-October 2024, pp. 79-83.

[5] "Drone in construction & infrastructure,"

https://www.jouav.com/industry/drone-in-construction

[6] "How drones work and how to fly them," May 2024,

https://dronelaunchacademy.com/resources/how-do-drones-work/

[7] "What are the main applications of drones?" June 2024,

https://www.jouav.com/blog/applications-of-drones.html

[8] "Drones in manufacturing: A game-changer for industry,"

https://viper-drones.com/industries/infrastructure-drone-use/manufacturing/#:~:text=The%20integration%20of%20drones%20into,on%20manufacturing%20is%20no%20exception.

[9] "How drones are helping musicians create better experiences for fans,"

https://agency.dottedmusic.com/tpost/85mn5h4b71-how-drones-are-helping-musicians-create

[10] "4 Innovative uses of drones in the entertainment industry,"

https://adam.edu.sg/4-innovative-uses-of-drones-in-the-entertainment-industry/?utm_source=rss&utm_medium=rss&utm_campaign=4-innovative-uses-of-drones-in-the-entertainment-industry

[11] "The impact of drones on the entertainment industry,"

https://www.embention.com/news/the-impact-of-drones-on-the-entertainment-industry/#:~:text=Drones%20in%20the%20cinema%20and,for%20expensive%20helicopters%20or%20cranes.

[12] "How is drone technology changing the media industry?" February 2024,

https://www.linkedin.com/pulse/how-drone-technology-changing-media-industry-appsierra-saqsf/

[13] K. Gallagher, "Drones for best supporting role in film & TV production," April 2016,

https://www.simulyze.com/blog/drones-for-best-supporting-role-in-film-tv-production

[14] M. Murison, "Drones and the future of entertainment," July 2017,

https://blog.zeitview.com/2017/07/10/drones-and-the-future-of-entertainment

[15] C. Opfer, "How are drones changing media coverage?"

https://people.howstuffworks.com/culture-traditions/tv-and-culture/drones-changing-media-coverage.htm

[16] "How drones are changing the entertainment industry,"

https://www.unitedrotorcraft.com/newsroom/how-drones-are-changing-the-entertainment-industry/

[17] "6 Benefits of using drones in corporate video production,"

https://mackmediagroup.com/6-benefits-of-using-drones-in-corporate-video-production/

[18] "Drone technology in the world of entertainment,"

https://dronemajor.net/editorials/drone-technology-in-the-world-of-entertainment

[19] "Journalism and technology: The use of drones for news gathering in Africa," December 2023,

https://www.cima.ned.org/blog/journalism-and-technology-the-use-of-drones-for-news-gathering-in-africa/

[20] "Aerial cinematography: The role of drones in film production," March 2024,

https://c-istudios.com/aerial-cinematography-the-role-of-drones-in-film-production/

[21] M. N. O. Sadiku, *Drones and Their Applications*. Xlibris, 2025.

[22] D. R. Faust, *Entertainment Drones (Drones: Eyes in the Skies)*. Powerkids Press, 2015.

[23] L. L. Bella, *Drones and Entertainment*. Rosen Publishing Group, Inc., 2016.

[24] P. Chamberlain, *Drones and Journalism: How the Media is Making Use of Unmanned Aerial Vehicles*. Taylor & Francis, 2017.

CHAPTER 5
BIG DATA IN
MEDIA AND ENTERTAINMENT

"Art is moral passion married to entertainment. Moral passion without entertainment is propaganda, and entertainment without moral passion is television."

— Rita Mae Brown

5.1 INTRODUCTION

Today, the term "media" encompasses not only television, radio and print, but also phone calls, text messaging, social platforms, and video chatting — any channel through which information and entertainment is disseminated. The media and entertainment industry is all about art and employing big data in it. Publishers, broadcasters, news organizations, cable companies, and gaming companies in the media and entertainment industry are facing new business models for the way they create, market, and distribute their content. This is happening because today's consumers search and access content anywhere, at any time, and on any device. For the media and entertainment industry, their customers are the real kings and big data is helping them to treat their customers like a one. With millions of digital consumers, media and entertainment companies are in a unique position to leverage their big data assets for more profitable customer engagement [1].

The media and entertainment industries have frequently been at the forefront of adopting new technologies. The exploitation of data in the media industry has always played an important role, especially nowadays, when people interact with various sources of information and spend more time online, producing data through their devices (smartphones, tablets, laptops, etc). Media platforms use big data to track content performance across various platforms, such as social media, streaming services, and websites. This can help companies identify trends and optimize their content strategy. For example, media companies like Disney track the performance of their movies and TV shows across various platforms to understand audience engagement and optimize their content strategy.

We are living in the era of big data, which is huge amounts of data in digital form. From healthcare to finance, big data is being used to transform how industries function, enabling business enterprises to create new revenue streams, enhance customer experiences, and increase operational efficiency. Big data plays a crucial role in the media and entertainment industry by enabling companies to understand audience behavior, personalize content, and optimize marketing efforts. It significantly impacts the media and entertainment industry by enabling data-driven decision-making, improving user experiences, and streamlining operations. It is now the real hero for the media and entertainment industry [2].

This chapter presents an overview of the state of the art of big data in the media and entertainment industry. It begins with explaining what big data is all about. It covers the characteristics of big data. It describes big data in media and entertainment and provides some examples. It discusses some applications of big data in the media and entertainment industry. It highlights the benefits and challenges of big data in media and entertainment. The last section concludes with comments.

5.2 WHAT IS BIG DATA?

Big data applies to data sets of extreme size (e.g. exabytes, zettabytes) which are beyond the capability of the commonly used software tools. It involves situation where very large data sets are big in volume, velocity, veracity, and variability [3]. The data is too big, too fast, or does not fit the regular database architecture. It may require different strategies and tools for profiling, measurement, assessment, and processing. Different components of big data are shown in Figure 5.1 [4]. The cloud word for big data is shown in Figure 5.2 [5].

Figure 5.1 Different components of big data [4].

Figure 5.2 The cloud word for big data [5].

Big Data is essentially classified into three types [6]:

• *Structured Data:* This is highly organized and is the easiest to work with. Any data that can be stored, accessed, and processed in the form of fixed format is known as a structured data. It may be stored in tabular format. Due to their nature, it is easy for programs to sort through and collect data. Structured data has quantitative data such as age, contact, address, billing, expenses, credit card numbers, etc. Data that is stored in a relational database management system is an example of structured data.

• *Unstructured Data:* This refers to unorganized data such as video files, log files, audio files, and image files. Any data with unknown form or the structure is classified as unstructured data. Almost everything generated by a computer is unstructured data. It takes a lot of time and effort required to make unstructured data readable. Examples of unstructured data include Metadata, Twitter tweets, and other social media posts.

• *Semi-structured Data:* This falls somewhere between structured data and unstructured data, i.e., both forms of data are present. Semi-structured data can be inherited such as location, time, email address, or device ID stamp.

The different types of big data are depicted in Figure 5.3 [7].

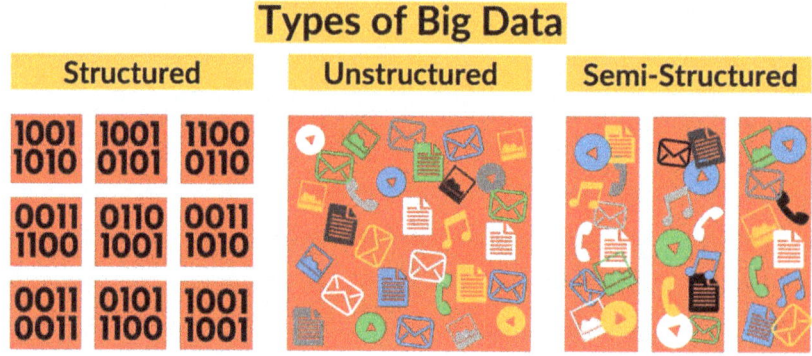

Figure 5.3 Types of big data [7].

The process of examining big data is often referred to big data analytics. It is an emerging field since massive computing capabilities have been made available by e-infrastructures [8]. Big data analytics is the application of advanced analytic techniques to large, heterogeneous data sets that comprise structured, semi-structured, and unstructured data from many sources with sizes ranging from terabytes to zettabytes.

Analytics include statistical models and other methods that are aimed at creating empirical predictions. Data-driven organizations use analytics to guide decisions at all levels. Several techniques have been proposed for analyzing big data. These include the

HACE theorem, cloud computing, Hadoop, and MapReduce [9].

5.3 CHARACTERISTICS OF BIG DATA

Big data is growing rapidly and expanding in all science and engineering, including physical, biological, and medical services. Different companies use different means to maintain their big data. As shown in Figure 5.4 [10], big data is characterized by 42 Vs. The first five Vs are volume, velocity, variety, veracity, and value .

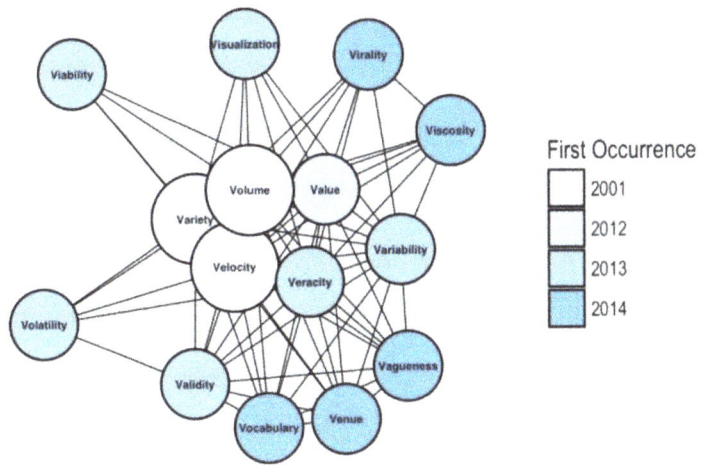

Figure 5.4 The 42 V's of big data [10].

- *Volume:* This refers to the size of the data being generated both inside and outside organizations and is increasing annually. Some regard big data as data over one petabyte in volume.

- *Velocity:* This depicts the unprecedented speed at which data are generated by Internet users, mobile users, social media, etc. Data are generated and processed in a fast way to extract useful, relevant information. Big data could be analyzed in real time, and it has movement and velocity.

- *Variety:* This refers to the data types since big data may originate from heterogeneous sources and is in different formats (e.g., videos, images, audio, text, logs). BD comprises of structured, semi-structured or unstructured data.

- *Veracity:* By this, we mean the truthfulness of data, i.e. weather the data comes from a reputable, trustworthy, authentic, and accountable source. It suggests the inconsistency in the quality of different sources of big data. The data may not be 100% correct.

- *Value:* This is the most important aspect of the big data. It is the desired outcome of big data processing. It refers to the process of discovering hidden values from large datasets. It denotes the value derived from the analysis of the existing data. If one cannot extract some business value from the data, there is no use managing and storing it.

On this basis, small data can be regarded as having low volume, low velocity, low variety, low veracity, and low value. Additional five Vs has been added [10]:

- *Validity:* This refers to the accuracy and correctness of data. It also indicates how up to date it is.

- *Viability:* This identifies the relevancy of data for each use case. Relevancy of data is required to maintain the desired and accurate outcome through analytical and predictive measures.

- *Volatility:* Since data are generated and change at a rapid rate, volatility determines how quickly data change.

- *Vulnerability:* The vulnerability of data is essential because privacy and security are of utmost importance for personal data.

- *Visualization:* Data needs to be presented unambiguously and attractively to the user. Proper visualization of large and complex clinical reports helps in finding valuable insights.

Instead of the 10V's above, some suggest the following 5V's: Venue, Variability, Vocabulary, Vagueness, and Validity) [11].

Industries that benefit from big data include the healthcare, financial, airline, travel, restaurants, automobile, sports, agriculture, and hospitality industries. Big data technologies are playing an essential role in farming: machines are equipped with sensors that measure data in their environment. Structured and unstructured data are generated in various types [12-15].

5.4 BIG DATA IN MEDIA AND ENTERTAINMENT

The media and entertainment industry is evolving constantly, and data analytics is emerging as a game-changer in shaping the landscape. It is evolving at an unprecedented rate, driven by the twin needs to reduce operating costs and simultaneously generate more revenue from increasingly competitive and uncertain markets. This transformational integration of big data and analytics is not just reshaping content creation and distribution but is also redefining the landscape of media and entertainment software development. The transformative impact of big data and analytics in the media and entertainment industry is enabling the industry to strategically use data analytics to reshape the industry in several key areas, drive innovation, and enhance user experiences. Figure 5.5 shows a representation of the media and entertainment industry [16].

Figure 5.5 A representation of the media and entertainment industry [16].

Over the past few years, big data has grown crucial in the media and entertainment industries. Entertainment businesses have obtained through insights into their clients, systems, and processes by embracing big data analytics. Big data in media and entertainment is not only assisting businesses to gain hidden insights into consumer behavior but is also helping the delivery of personalized content. Today, we can have access to our favorite shows and movies anytime, anywhere with the advancements of services by using big data analytics. We now have access to everything at our fingertips and big data has been the backbone of this amazing transformation. Because of this, technological development has become essential in bringing outside entertainment to consumers' homes.

5.5 EXAMPLES OF BIG DATA IN MEDIA AND ENTERTAINMENT

Big data in the media industry is a big deal. The most competitive media companies are adopting big data solutions to help manage their data, generate new insights, and improve their services. For example, the most pre-eminent players in the media and entertainment industry, such as Netflix, Amazon, Hulu, and Disney, have already been leveraging big data as part of their operations to enhance the customer experience. The following are examples of such companies [17]:

• *Spotify* is a music streaming service using listening data to curate personalized experiences for its users. Spotify has more 80 million users, which translates to a ton of listening data. So much data, in fact, that Spotify has a blog that displays the different ways data is understood on the platform.

• *Instagram* is a social platform that connects users through photos and videos. Acquired by Facebook in 2012, the widely used site has upwards of one billion users. That means it also has mountains of data. Instagram offers many kinds of profiles, including business profiles that offer users data insights about things like the reach of individual posts, past post comparisons, and the origins of audience impressions.

• *Ampersand* is a digital advertising solution specializing in targeted TV ads. The company manages and analyzes large volumes of data to ensure effective targeting and campaign optimization. Ampersand works to equip advertisers with insights and solutions to help them make data-driven decisions that maximize the impact of their advertising campaigns.

• *NBCUniversal* is a titan of media and entertainment that captivates audiences with shows and movies distributed through an array of network television, film studio, and streaming brands. Data plays an important role in NBCUniversal's business strategy. The company leverages analytics tools to access user insights that inform decision making — an approach that has led to increased viewership.

• *Hulu* is a streaming service that provides access to a library of TV shows and movies, original content, and current seasons of television series airing on stations like FOX, ABC, and NBC. Accessible across devices, Hulu regularly adds content and recently expanded to offer a live TV service.

• *Netflix's* leadership in the marketplace can be directly attributed to successfully harnessing the power of big data. Big data and a robust analytics program have been a competitive advantage for Netflix over the past decade. With over 200 million subscribers, Netflix leverages its wealth of audience data to deliver personalized content recommendations and platform experiences. As the world's most popular streaming platform, Netflix analyzes its financial data to forecast demand for content, estimate its financial impact, and invest dollars to bring audiences the content they want.

5.6 APPLICATIONS OF BIG DATA IN MEDIA AND ENTERTAINMENT

The integration of big data and analytics is foundational to the new era in the entertainment industry. Various areas where big data can be used in media and entertainment include consumer care, advertising, content monetization, and data journalism. Figure 5.6 shows some use cases of big data analytics in M&E industry [18]. Common applications of big data in the M&E industry include the following [19-21]:

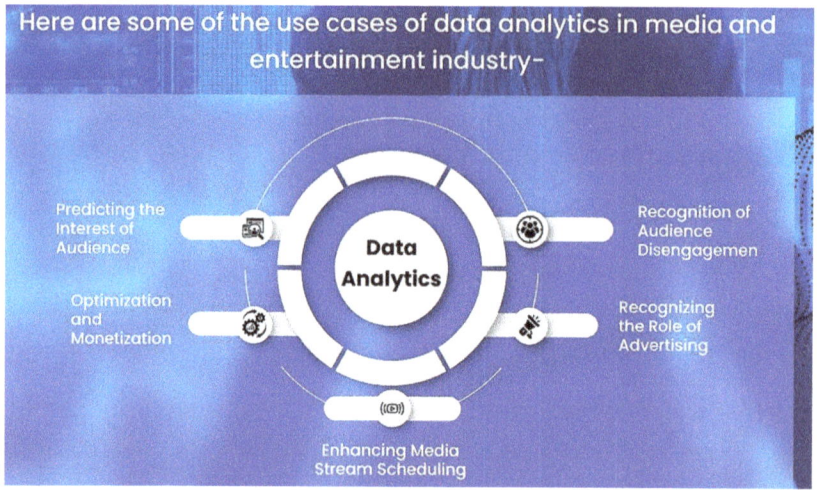

Figure 5.6 Some use cases of big data analytics in M&E industry [18].

• *Customer Care:* For a media and entertainment company, nobody is more important for them than its users and keeping its users happy is their toughest task. Companies need to ensure that they fulfill each of their customer's wishes. To attain the same, they must be aware of what their customers need. Big data analytics are used to recommend users shows or movies according to their preferences. Companies can even gain in-depth details about the other important things such as viewing history, ratings, reviews, data from social media, etc. Big data analytics is helping companies to connect with their customers in a much better way than they ever did.

• *Advertising:* Running a media and entertainment company without advertising is like winking at a person in the dark; you know what you are doing, but nobody else does. Advertising to media and entertainment companies is what food is to soul. A media company's success heavily depends on their advertising strategies. Big data helps media companies target advertisements more effectively by understanding consumer demographics, interests, and online behavior. Big data analysis helps companies to develop more personalized ads and provides insights about the best time to stream those ads to seek the attention of the maximum number of customers. As big data has made it possible for the media houses to understand their customer's exact preferences; it is quite easy for them to engross the customers.

• *Content Monetization:* Like all businesses, media companies aim to maximize revenue, minimize costs, and improve decision-making and business processes. As consumer interests shift from analog to digital media, there are substantial opportunities to monetize content and to identify new products and services. Entertainment and media companies can use big data to understand what content, products and features consumers want. Product updates have become more cost effective and time effective, thanks to the analysis of customer data. You will never know what features your consumers want or need you to release if you do not dive into the data; it could give you a competitive edge, increase revenue, and brand loyalty.

• *Data Analysis:* Media and entertainment companies generate and collect data from a variety of sources. They need to analyze data not only at the customer and product levels, but also at network and infrastructure levels. Audience data breaks down into three broad categories: personal data, demographic data, and behavioral data. Key technologies in the coming years will be descriptive analytics, more sophisticated customer relationship management solutions, and lastly data visualization solutions that are accessible to a wide range of users in the enterprise. It is only by "humanizing" these tools that big data will be able to deliver the benefits that data-driven businesses increasingly demand.

• *Data Journalism:* Journalism incorporated big data into its practices in a way that influenced the internal logic of the profession. In the last 30 years, digital technologies with the introduction of various tools have made journalistic work easier. However, they have also made journalist work more difficult, because they have overwhelmed journalists with more information than can be handled by their investigative toolboxes. Data journalism emerges as a result of these changes, and it is related to data-driven journalism. Specifically, the introduction of information and communications technology (ICT) and the availability big data have turned data journalism into its current form. Data journalism promotes open journalism and open data. The term open data is related to transparency, accountability, accessibility, and free, public, and recyclable use.

• *Audience Participation:* Although audience participation has always been part of the journalism practice, the diffusion of Web 2.0 tools along with the socio-economic circumstances have led to the proliferation of user-generated content and increased users' involvement in the news production process. Audience participation in news production can be enabled by data journalism projects as well. Thanks to the participation of victims and witnesses, a number of media organizations in Latin America have revealed situations involving huge breaches of human rights not identified in official records. Figure 5.7 shows an example of audience participation [22].

Figure 5.7 An example of audience participation [22].

• *Data Mining:* While it is clearly evident that there are multitudes of potential applications for big data in the media industry, the fact remains that these datasets are so large and complex that in practice they are particularly unwieldy. Data mining is defined as a logical procedure used in order to search through very big amounts of data, with the purpose of discovering new, non-trivial information, which can subsequently be used to arrive at previously unknown conclusions. By this definition, it is immediately obvious that data mining and big data go hand-in-hand when it comes to journalistic practices. As stated before, the nature of big data renders them inaccessible to being processed by humans, or even by simple software, because of various factors that make them hard to understand and compute.

5.7 BENEFITS

Integrating big data and analytics into the media and entertainment industry is laying the foundation of a new era. As these technologies continue to evolve, they are set to unlock more possibilities for creating engaging and innovative entertainment experiences. Big data in the media industry can yield three different types of insights: diagnostic, predictive, and prescriptive. By using big data analytics, entertainment companies have been able to gain detailed insights regarding not only their customers but also their systems and processes. Other benefits of big data in the M&E industry include the following [18,23]:

• *Personalized Content:* By analyzing viewer's viewing habits, preferences, and interactions, these technologies will enable entertainment platforms to design content that resonates with individual tastes.

• *Informed Decision-making:* Data analytics presents deep insights into viewer preferences, demographics, and behaviors, thereby equipping content creators and distributors with valuable insights for informed decision-making. This data is instrumental in shaping content strategies, scheduling releases, and guiding the creation of new content as per audience demands.

• *Predictive Analysis:* This helps anticipate future trends and viewer preferences, enabling the sector to stay ahead of the curve. By predicting potential successes, media and entertainment studios can make informed decisions about different projects, thus reducing the financial risks associated with content production.

• *Prescriptive Insights:* These are recommendations to make a business decision or take action in a certain way. Prescriptive insights are also the domain of artificial intelligence, requiring the AI application to translate its forecasts into actionable recommendations that support strategic business objectives. Media companies who leverage AI to analyze their big data can generate more accurate and higher-quality insights than those who stick to manual methods

• *Data Management:* Data management, including aggregation and normalization, is a time-consuming task for media companies who still depend on manual processes. Enterprise AI solutions with multi-platform integration features can streamline and automate the process of aggregating data from multiple sources into a centralized repository and normalizing the data to prepare it for analytics.

• *Targeted Marketing:* With detailed audience insights, organizations can create highly targeted marketing campaigns to resonate with specific viewer segments. This level of targeting will help enhance viewer engagement while ensuring a higher return on investment for marketing campaigns.

• *Advertising:* The primary factor determining a company's market worth and profitability is still advertising. Advertisements seem to be a natural component of any entertainment industry. This assists the businesses in acting as retargeting agents so that advertising will appear if people are watching a show or a movie with a connection to the items. Big data applications assist in analyzing user behavior and what they are likely to buy through targeted advertisements.

• *Content Optimization:* This is the ongoing practice of maximizing revenue from content distribution and licensing agreements. Enterprise AI solutions can help media companies forecast audience demand and assess the revenue potential of various types of content. As a result, media companies can make better strategic decisions about licensing or producing content and distribution teams can leverage insights to maximize licensing terms.

• *Revenue:* Another crucial aspect where big data has proven to be invaluable is revenue. It analyzes what customers want, what is in vogue in the market, the target audience's viewing history, etc. to offer recommendations about generating better sales, adapting marketing strategies, fine-tune the when and where of content delivery, etc. All these measures seek to ensure high customer engagement rates and thus, better revenue for the company. Media organizations realized that by studying content consumption data, they can extract useful information which may help in designing successful publishing strategies and lead to new revenue opportunities.

5.8 CHALLENGES

In spite of its benefits, integrating big data and analytics in entertainment software development comes with challenges, including data privacy concerns, managing vast data volumes, and ensuring data accuracy. Most media firms are already doing some big data analytics, but the technical challenges of efficiently pooling data from multiple sources and extracting insights may be preventing them from using their data to its full potential. Attracting and keeping customers engaged are the biggest challenges faced by media and entertainment companies across the world. Big data as a phenomena is still, by their very nature, hard to access and work. Other challenges of big data in the M&E industry include the following [23]:

• *Siloed Data:* Big data in the media industry may be collected from subscribers, generated internally and stored in a database, provided by distribution partners, or sourced from a third-party organization. These multiple sources of data live in separate systems (data silos), and this segmentation means they cannot easily be integrated for analytics applications.

• *Non-standardized Formats:* Big data in the entertainment industry comes from multiple sources and may be in a variety of different formats. A media firm that licenses content to ten different distributors might receive ten different profit-sharing reports, each with their own fields and format. The lack of a standardized format means that this data must be normalized before it can be analyzed effectively.

- *Manual Data Processes:* While some media companies are using complex algorithms to process big data, others are still dependent on manual processes for data aggregation, normalization, analytics, and reporting. But as big data continues to grow, manual processes become more time-consuming, insights are delayed, and the overall impact and value of big data diminishes.

- *Ethical Considerations:* It is crucial for media companies to use big data responsibly and ethically, ensuring that data is used to benefit users and not exploit them.

- *Infrastructure:* While start-ups and SMEs can operate efficiently with open source and cloud infrastructure, for larger, older players, updating legacy IT infrastructure is a challenge. Legacy products and standards still need to be supported in the transition to big data ways of thinking and working. Failure to transform the culture and skillset of staff could impact companies who are profitable today but cannot adapt to data-driven business models.

- *Consumer Awareness:* There is increased consumer awareness and concern about how personal data is being used. There is regulatory uncertainty for European businesses that handle personal data, which potentially puts them at a disadvantage compared to, say, US companies who operate within a much more relaxed legal landscape.

5.9 CONCLUSION

Media and entertainment industry is advancing at an unprecedented, governed by dual requirements to minimize costs while at the same time generating more revenues from a highly competitive and uncertain market. The media and entertainment sector is in many respects an early adopter of big data technologies, but much more evolution has to happen for the full potential to be realized. The sector is experiencing a significant transformation with the integration of big data and analytics. Big data and analytics are key drivers for industry growth, extending beyond content personalization to strategic decision-making and significantly influencing the entertainment sector's overall success.

With the influence of big data and analytics in media and entertainment on the rise, it is becoming evident that these technologies are pivotal to the industry's future trajectory. The future of entertainment is here, and it is decidedly data-driven. More information about big data in the media and entertainment industry can be found in the books in [24-26] and the following related journal: *Journal of Big Data.*

REFERENCES

[1] "Big data in media and entertainment,"

https://www.qubole.com/big-data-in-media-and-entertainment

[2] M. N. O. Sadiku, P. A. Adekunte, and J. O. Sadiku, "Big data in media and entertainment," *International Journal of Trend in Scientific Research and Development*, vol. 9, no. 3, May-June 2025, pp. 875-884.

[3] M. N. O. Sadiku, M. Tembely, and S.M. Musa, "Big data: An introduction for engineers," *Journal of Scientific and Engineering Research*, vol. 3, no. 2, 2016, pp. 106-108.

[4] A. Slamecka, "Big data explosion," April 2022,

https://blogs.cisco.com/financialservices/big-data-explosion

[5] "Passion points: Analytics in the sports, media & entertainment industries," February 2017,

https://gradblog.schulich.yorku.ca/event/passion-points-analytics-in-the-sports-media-entertainment-industries/

[6] "The complete overview of big data,"

https://intellipaat.com/blog/tutorial/hadoop-tutorial/big-data-overview/

[7] R. Allen, "Types of big data | Understanding & Interacting with key types (2024),"

https://investguiding-com.custommapposter.com/article/types-of-big-data-understanding-amp-interacting-with-key-types

[8] P. Baumann et al., "Big data analytics for earth sciences: The earthserver approach," *International Journal of Digital Earth*, vol. 19, no. 1, 2016, pp.3-29.

[9] X. Wu et al., "Knowledge engineering with big data," *IEEE Intelligent Systems*, September/October 2015, pp.46-55.

[10] "The 42 V's of big data and data science,"

https://www.kdnuggets.com/2017/04/42-vs-big-data-data-science.html

[11] P. K. D. Pramanik, S. Pal, and M. Mukhopadhyay, "Healthcare big data: A comprehensive overview," in N. Bouchemal (ed.), *Intelligent Systems for Healthcare Management and Delivery*. IGI Global, chapter 4, 2019, pp. 72-100.

[12] J. Moorthy et al., "Big data: Prospects and challenges," *The Journal for Decision Makers*, vol. 40, no. 1, 2015, pp. 74–96.

https://www.grandviewresearch.com/industry-analysis/industrial-wireless-sensor-networks-iwsn-market

[13] A. K. Tiwari, H. Chaudhary, and S. Yadav, "A review on big data and its security," *Proceedings of IEEE Sponsored 2nd International Conference on Innovations in Information Embedded and Communication Systems*, 2015.

[14] M. B. Hoy, "Big data: An introduction for librarians," *Medical Reference Services Quarterly*, vol. 33, no 3. 2014, pp. 320-326.

[15] M. Viceconti, P. Hunter, and R. Hose, "Big data, big knowledge: Big data for personalized healthcare," *IEEE Journal of Medical and Health Informatics*, vol. 19, no. 4, July 2015, pp. 1209-1215.

[16] R. Williamson, "Media and entertainment: How this industry is impacted by big data," January 2021,

https://www.datasciencecentral.com/media-and-entertainment-how-this-industry-is-impacted-by-big-data/

[17] A. Schroer, "Big data in media & entertainment: 15 examples to know," August 2024,

https://builtin.com/articles/big-data-media

[18] "Data analytics in media and entertainment (M&E) industry,"

https://www.sganalytics.com/blog/data-analytics-in-media-and-entertainment-industry/

[19] "Big data in media and entertainment – The new hero in industry,"

https://data-flair.training/blogs/big-data-in-media-and-entertainment/

[20] "5 Ways big data plays a major role in the media and entertainment industry," July 2018,

https://www.maropost.com/blog/5-ways-big-data-plays-a-major-role-in-the-media-and-entertainment-industry/

[21] A. Veglis et al., "Applications of big data in media organizations," *Social Sciences*, vol. 11, no. 9. 2022.

[22] "Data-driven decisions: How big data and analytics are shaping the future of media & entertainment," April 2024,

https://www.sprinterra.com/data-driven-decisions-how-big-data-and-analytics-are-shaping-the-future-of-media-entertainment/

[23] "5 AI-Driven use cases for big data in media & entertainment," October 2022,

https://www.symphonyai.com/resources/blog/media/5-ai-driven-use-cases-for-big-data-in-media-entertainment/

[24] M. N. O. Sadiku, U. C. Chukwu, and P. O. Adebo, *Big Data and Its Applications*. Moldova, Europe: Lambert Academic Publishing, 2024.

[25] P. C. K. Hung, *Big Data Applications and Use Cases (International Series on Computer, Entertainment and Media Technology)*. Springer, 2016.

[26] T. Hennig-Thurau and M. B. Houston, *Entertainment Science: Data Analytics and Practical Theory for Movies, Games, Books, and Music*. Springer, 2018.

CHAPTER 6
CLOUD COMPUTING IN MEDIA AND ENTERTAINMENT

"Excellence is attained when you care more than others think is wise; risk more than others think is safe; dream more than others think is practical; expect more than others think is possible."

— Jim Gentil

6.1 INTRODUCTION

The entertainment sector is a huge umbrella term involving a large number of sub-industries devoted to entertainment. It is the industry that always provides fun, entertainment, enjoyment, and amusement to people. It includes but not limited to television programs, movies, broadcast, radio, books, video games, and special events wherein live streaming of content is seen. The US media and entertainment industry is the largest in the world and accounts to one-third of this industry [1]. Figure 6.1 shows a typical media and entertainment live event [2].

Figure 6.1 A typical media and entertainment live event [2].

Cloud computing has become a game-changer, offering seamless access to data anytime, anywhere. As technology evolves, cloud technology becomes increasingly crucial in driving innovation across industries, from aviation to healthcare, gaming, technology, and finance. Cloud computing has revolutionized business operations, and the media and entertainment (M&E) sector is no exception. With the rise of cloud computing, innovations in the entertainment industry have come to the fore. Cloud computing has also revolutionized the way we listen to music and podcasts. The cloud makes media processing faster, more efficient, and more accessible.

Cloud computing has revolutionized the dynamics of the entertainment business by making accessible the tools and infrastructure required for efficient content creation, management, and distribution. It is reshaping content creation, distribution, and consumption. Cloud computing in the media allows new ways of creating, managing, and broadcasting media content more effectively. Along with easy collaboration, sophisticated workflow, and data management, cloud resources have prevented huge data losses and generated high-quality content. The adaptive nature of cloud offerings makes it a perfect choice for the M&E industry that is currently looking for ways to address the emerging global shifts in media and entertainment patterns [3,4].

This chapter examines the various roles of cloud computing in the media and entertainment sector. It begins with explaining the basics of cloud computing. It describes cloud computing in the media and entertainment industry and provides some applications. It highlights the benefits and challenges of cloud computing in media and entertainment. The last section concludes with comments.

6.2 CLOUD COMPUTING BASICS

Cloud computing represents a newly emerging service-oriented computing technology. It is the provision of scalable computing resources as a service over the Internet. It allows manufacturers to use many forms of new production systems such as 3D printing, high-performance computing (HPC), industrial Internet of things (IIoT), and industrial robots. It is transforming virtually every facet of modern manufacturing. It is innovating, reducing cost, and bolstering the competitiveness of American manufacturing [5]. Figure 6.2 shows the symbol for cloud computing [6]. Some features of cloud computing are displayed in Figure 6.3 [7].

Figure 6.2 The symbol for cloud computing [6].

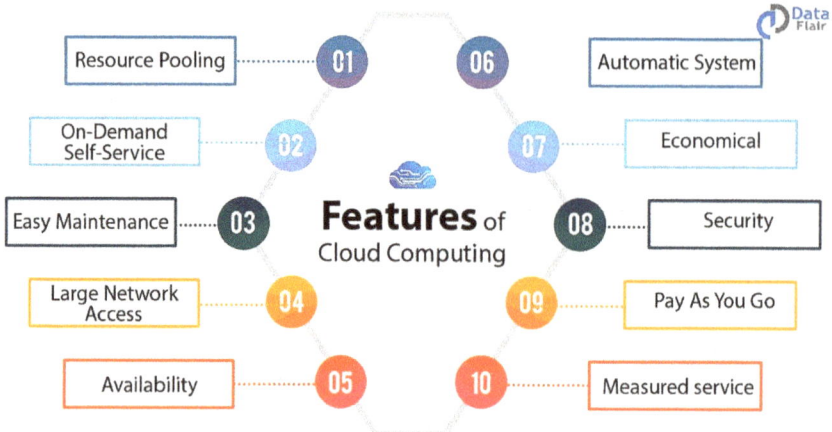

Figure 6.3 Some features of cloud computing [7].

The key characteristic of cloud computing is the virtualization of computing resources and services. Cloud computing is implemented in one of three major formats: software as a service (SAAS), platform as a service (PAAS), or infrastructure as a service (IAAS). These services are explained as follows:

SaaS: This is a software delivery model in which software and associated data are hosted on the cloud. In this model, cloud service providers offer on-demand access to computing resources such as virtual machines and cloud storage.

PaaS allows the end-user to create a software solution using tools or libraries from the platform service provider. In this model, cloud service providers deliver computing platforms such as programming and execution.

In the IaaS model, cloud service providers can rent manufacturing equipment such as 3D printers.

Just like cloud computing, CM services can be categorized into three major deployment models (public, private, and hybrid clouds) [8]:

- Private cloud refers to a centralized management effort in which manufacturing services are shared within one company or its subsidiaries. A private cloud is often used exclusively by one organization, possibly with multiple business units.

• Public cloud realizes the key concept of sharing services with the general public. Public clouds are commonly implemented through data centers operated by providers such as Amazon, Google, IBM, and Microsoft.

• Hybrid cloud that spans multiple configurations. and is a composed of two or more clouds (private, community or public), offering the benefits of multiple deployment modes.

These services and models are shown in Figure 6.4 [9]. Cloud computing finds application in almost every field.

Types of Cloud Computing

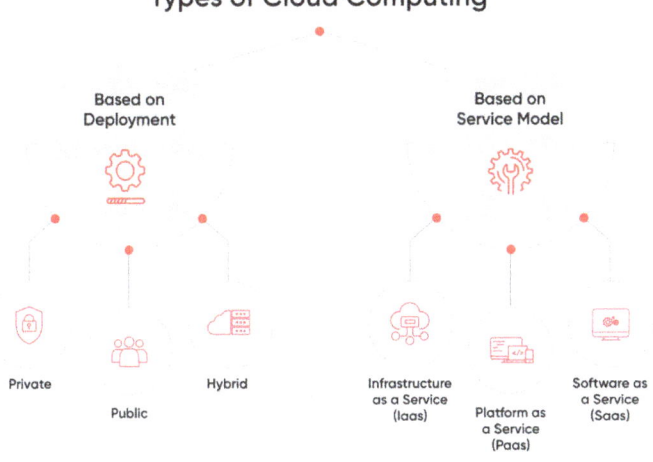

Figure 6.4 Cloud computing services and models [9].

6.3 CLOUD COMPUTING IN MEDIA AND ENTERTAINMENT

Modern technology has leveled the playing field between large enterprises and upstarts, unlocked new opportunities, and intensified competition. With these changes, consumers expect more from media and entertainment companies. Consumers are fast changing their preferences towards digital media channels with the rising on-demand content being consumed through Internet-connected devices—their phones, smart TVs, tablets, computers, set-top boxes, gaming consoles, and digital media players, as compared to more traditional forms of media such as TV, print, and radio. Providing on-demand content to the consumer at such speed has necessitated media and entertainment (M&E) companies to move away from legacy productions systems. The adaptive nature of cloud offerings makes it a perfect choice for the M&E industry that is currently looking for ways to address the emerging global shifts in media and entertainment patterns. The adoption of a cloud-based ecosystem can help these companies find success in this dynamic technology landscape [10]. Cloud computing in media and entertainment industry will totally transform the landscape, enabling creators to deliver top-notch content and even invent new forms of entertainment. Figure 6.5 shows a representation of cloud computing in the M&E industry [11].

Figure 6.5 A representation of cloud computing in the M&E industry [11].

Cloud technology has become an essential tool for many businesses. The demand for cloud computing in media and entertainment has been increasing because it is commonly used. The scalability, flexibility, and other advanced features make it easy to have a stable and scalable infrastructure. By using cloud computing, M&E companies are developing new and better ways to quickly and efficiently deliver rich content to a fine-grained targeted audience.

6.4 APPLICATIONS OF CLOUD COMPUTING IN MEDIA AND ENTERTAINMENT

Cloud computing and AI have changed the media and entertainment industry forever. Cloud computing can help shape the future landscape of media and entertainment.

The media and entertainment industry can use cloud computing in various ways. These include streaming, audio recording, asset management, archive storage, etc. Common areas of applications of cloud computing in M&E industry include the following [12]:

• *Media Streaming:* Traditional TV has become obsolete. Viewers now want the freedom to watch what they want, when they want it. This is possible due to smart TVs, media cloud processing, and streaming services. Streaming services and streaming media have changed how we watch TV, movies, and videos. Media streaming is the linchpin of how we consume media today. Over-the-top (OTT) streaming services allow media companies to provide content directly to customers over the Internet, eliminating the need for a system operator. Media streaming is a way of delivering media over the Internet in real time. Unlike downloads, where you wait for the whole file, cloud based streaming lets you start playing right away. The media streaming services, through cloud computing, can scale and deliver high-quality content on multiple devices.

• *Targeted Advertising:* Through cloud-driven ad platforms, media outfits can precisely target their advertising campaigns with unparalleled accuracy. By analyzing user behavior patterns, demographics data points, and content consumption trends, marketers can tailor their ad strategies for enhanced engagement levels, leading to better returns on investment. Cloud computing can help shape the future landscape of media and entertainment. If you are thinking of getting into this vibrant industry, understanding how cloud technologies can be leveraged is paramount for success.

• *Cloud Media Processing:* Cloud media processing involves the manipulation of various media content, incorporating video, audio, and images. The aim of audio, video, and image processing is the conversion of these files into different formats so that they can be used efficiently and smoothly. Cloud-based image processing refers to running information through computerized algorithms so that we can analyze the image and discover meaningful insights from it. Image processing requires substantial storage and cloud image processing fulfills this need by providing extensive storage space and processing capabilities. This is the reason for the gaining popularity of cloud-based image processing. Video processing is primarily a sequence of images. However, the resulting signal is still a video stream.

6.5 BENEFITS

Cloud computing can offer countless benefits for a business of any size. It has the power to revolutionize various aspects of the M&E industry. By harnessing cloud computing capabilities, companies can offer personalized and immersive encounters to their audience. One of the major benefits of the cloud in the media and entertainment industry is how it enables global content delivery. Companies can now serve content to users worldwide in multiple formats. Organizations can go directly to the consumer, without compromising security. Other benefits of cloud computing in media and entertainment include the following [13,14]:

• *Scalability:* Cloud platforms are designed to be scalable. Cloud computing scalability matters because it ensures consistent performance during peak usage periods, maintaining user satisfaction. Cloud platforms offer on-demand and flexible resources, allowing media companies to scale up or down as needed. This allows services to never go down during sudden traffic spikes during the release of some popular show or event. This is crucial for handling fluctuating demand and ensuring seamless streaming experiences.

• *Personalizing Experiences:* This is one of the mainstays that have revolutionized the whole aspect of video streaming. Cloud computing enables over-the-top (OTT) platforms to harness data analytics, offering highly personalized user experiences. This personalized content not only enhances user engagement but also improves satisfaction by delivering more relevant and appealing content suggestions, keeping viewers hooked and driving higher retention rates. Figure 6.6 shows personalizing experiences on screens [13].

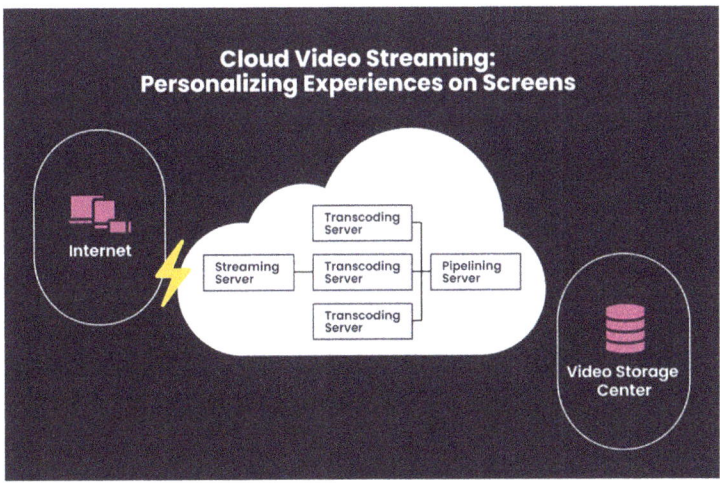

Figure 6.6 Personalizing experiences on screens [13].

• *Reduced Costs:* Building an on-premise infrastructure to support the high performance, high-resolution media files is cost-prohibitive. Not only must companies invest in server and storage hardware, but they must also pay for employees to manage the large data centers. Moving to the cloud allows organizations to tune up their big data storage strategy in a cost effective way. No hardware is necessary when using a cloud solutions provider. Rising costs in other areas of the industry can be offset by deploying a more cost-effective cloud solution.

• *Collaboration:* Cloud-based platforms facilitate collaboration among teams, regardless of location, enabling remote work and efficient project management. Cloud platforms facilitate seamless collaboration across worldwide teams, which is particularly beneficial for media projects requiring international cooperation. Image processing has made it possible for teams to work in real-time collaboration, thus allowing smooth work on any visual project and even collaboration across locations. Photographers and designers can now start or continue projects from anywhere, enhancing flexibility and fostering collaboration throughout the creative process.

• *Flexibility:* Cloud computing offers a great deal of flexibility. M&E companies need flexibility in storage configurations to move files quickly, whether in the cloud or on-premise. They need the ability to seamlessly adjust storage requirements based on specific use cases. Entertainment companies can scale up or down their use of cloud-based services as needed without having to make any major changes to their infrastructure. With the ability to adjust storage from any location, entertainment companies can gain the flexibility they need to operate cost effectively.

• *Meeting Customer Expectations:* Consumers expect high-quality digital content. They expect to access what they want when they want it. For media companies, the ups and downs of customer expectations make it difficult to plan storage requirements. Since viewership can change in seconds, using the cloud in the media and entertainment industry provides a scalable solution that is agile enough to meet changes in real time.

• *Enhanced Security:* Speed and security are the two most important elements for the media and entertainment industry. With more digital assets being stored in multiple locations, cybersecurity becomes a crucial part of business continuity. Cyberattacks can bring operations to a halt, so cloud storage platforms should have a strong security posture. Cloud computing offers stronger security measures, such as encryption and multi-factor authentication, which help safeguard valuable media content from unauthorized access and cyberattacks.

• *Sustainability:* Cloud providers that utilize renewable energy contribute to greater energy efficiency, making cloud computing more environmentally friendly than traditional data centers.

• Global Reach: Cloud hosting facilitates global distribution with instant availability. It makes it easy for content producers and streaming platforms to reach audiences worldwide. This expands audience bases, driving growth opportunities beyond traditional boundaries. Cloud-based streaming services and content delivery networks (CDNs) ensure content is accessible worldwide with minimal buffering and latency.

• *Low Latency:* In the broadcasting industry, high streaming performance with minimal delays and downtime is crucial to meet both user experience and expectations of the advertiser. On-premise servers are located on the media company's premises, while cloud media servers can be anywhere in the world. This way, cloud-based content providers can deliver media that streams to viewers using the closest best server, which reduces latency and improves user experience.

6.6 CHALLENGES

The M&E industry has to go through multiple challenges. Firstly, entertainment involves live streaming of content. To seamlessly stream content, media companies have to spend a lot of budget on bandwidth and other data management resources. Secondly, the traffic is unpredictable. When a video goes viral, you can expect millions of hits within minutes. So, media companies should be able to instantly scale up resources [1]. Another important challenge in the entertainment industry is personalization. While the vast majority of organizations in the media and entertainment industry are aware of the data explosion, few are adequately prepared to address the challenges. Other challenges include the following [15,16]:

• *Storage:* Data size is quickly outpacing storage space in the media and entertainment industry, and object-based storage can play a pivotal supporting role to help companies meet growing challenges. The media and entertainment industry is generating denser data types than it ever has before, and the density is accelerating at a rapid pace. Every day, media producers are creating more 4K and 8K content to meet the consumer demand for a better visual experience, but this trend exponentially increases storage costs for the companies that must preserve that content. As the industry continues to innovate and create, storage will play an integral role in helping digital assets be properly preserved, secured and accessed. Companies that are not up-to-speed on advancements in storage technology are facing major challenges because data growth in the media and entertainment industry shows no signs of slowing down. Organizations need to start looking at storage solutions that can carry them into the future. Figure 6.7 shows growing adoption of cloud storage by media and entertainment [17].

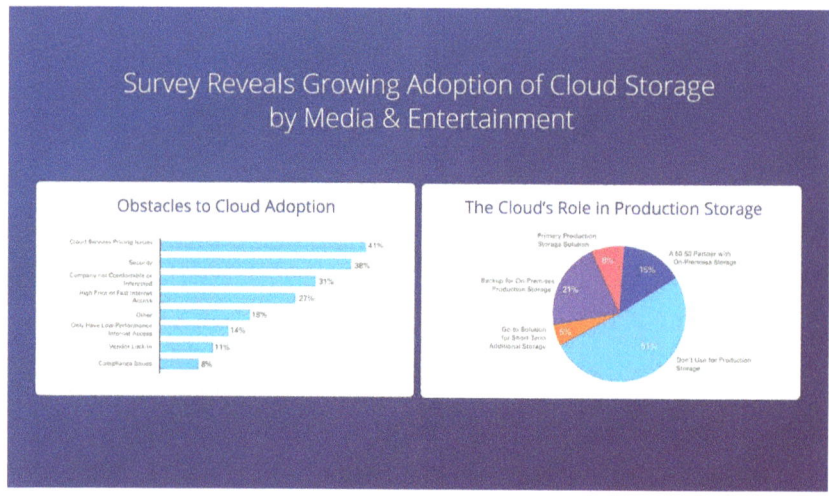

Figure 6.7 Growing adoption of cloud storage by media and entertainment [17].

• *Remote Working:* This a major challenge. Companies adopting widespread remote working during the pandemic were surprised by just how productive their teams were despite being at home. Intelligent transition and application of cloud managed services not only enable innovations but also address challenges of remote working like loss of data, poor content quality, etc.

• *Security:* Like many other branches of technology, security is a pressing concern in cloud-based computing. Security risks for cloud replicate those found in everyday activities with mobile devices, home computing, work compute environments, and daily life. M&E organizations have significant concerns about data security in the cloud, including the lack of native security services, backup/disaster recovery tools, and adequate security training for staff. They also worry about potential cloud security breaches and data loss or theft. Unauthorized access or piracy are possible with video streaming. Technologies for digital rights management

(DRM) can be used to prevent material theft and guarantee that only authorized users can view the video.

• *Sensitive Data:* This is another major concern. Sensitive data is defined as information that, if disclosed, misused or accessed without authorization, could result in harm, discrimination or adverse consequences for the individual to whom the data pertains. Organizations operating with highly sensitive data (in the cloud or on the ground) should consider encryption to prevent unauthorized parties from accessing it.

• *Cost Management:* Spending can be a significant challenge. Be certain your financial officers are prepared for the sometimes rapidly changing cost structures and "bring them along" in the process. Predicting and managing cloud costs can be difficult, especially with unpredictable usage patterns and potential over-provisioning or under-provisioning of resources.

• *Expertise and Training:* Finding the right experts to help with cloud implementations can be challenging. A lack of skilled personnel with experience in cloud computing and security can hinder cloud adoption and implementation. The skills gap is one of the biggest challenges for cloud computing technologies. These individuals are hard to find, sometimes hard to engage and can be costly to employ.

• *Vendor Lock-in:* Organizations may face challenges transitioning to different cloud providers if they become overly reliant on a single vendor's services. Businesses using cloud computing are ill-advised to become dependent on a specific single vendor, making it difficult to switch providers should something unforeseen occur.

• *Complexity:* Cloud computing can be complex, especially for businesses new to the technology, requiring a significant investment in time and resources to learn and implement cloud solutions. Be prepared for a lengthy startup period and engage a solutions architect who is experienced in what you do and with various cloud provider solutions. Integrating cloud solutions with existing legacy systems and workflows can be a complex and time-consuming process.

• *Network Dependence:* Reliant on a stable and reliable Internet connection for access to cloud resources, which can be a challenge in areas with limited bandwidth or network outages.

• *Compliance:* Navigating complex regulations and ensuring data privacy and residency in the cloud can be challenging for M&E companies.

• *Interoperability:* Ensuring that cloud-based systems and services can effectively interact with legacy systems and various tools within the M&E workflow can be a challenge.

Some of these challenges are shown in Figure 6.8 [16].

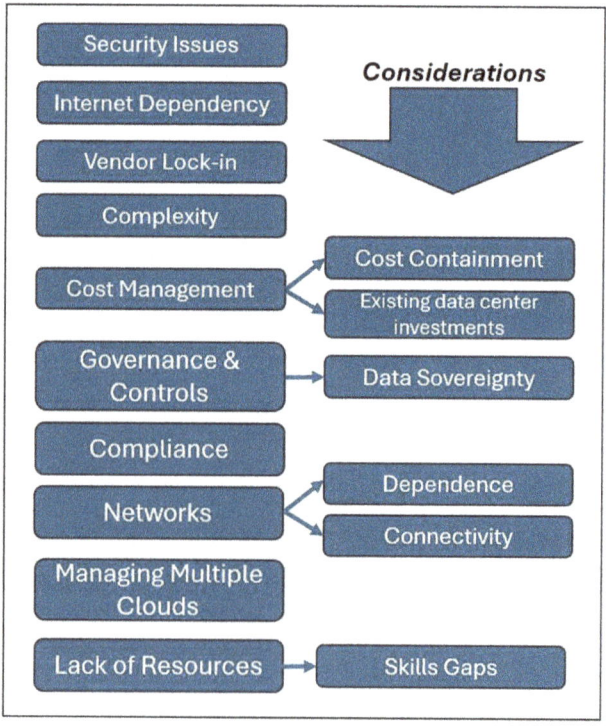

Figure 6.8 . Some challenges of cloud computing in M&E [16]

6.7 CONCLUSION

Cloud computing has significantly impacted the media and entertainment industry, offering solutions for content creation, distribution, and management. A firm's open-mindedness towards the adoption of cloud computing will give it a strategic advantage in such a dynamic and competitive environment. The time is now for the M&E industry players to join the bandwagon and deliver content the way consumers are demanding. M&E companies are increasingly eyeing the cloud platform to achieve their production, distribution, and archiving goals. With the aim of reducing IT operational costs and providing anytime and anywhere accessible high quality content will trigger the adoption of cloud solutions by media and entertainment firms globally. More information about cloud computing in the media and entertainment industry can be found in the following related journals:

- *Journal of Cloud Computing*
- *IEEE Cloud Computing*
- *IEEE Transactions on Cloud Computing*
- *International Journal of Cloud Applications and Computing*
- *International Journal of Cloud Computing and Services Science*
- *i-manager's Journal on Cloud Computing*

REFERENCES

[1] "How cloud is shaping the media and entertainment sector?" https://www.centerserv.com/Private-Sector/Media-And-Entertainment-Sector

[2] "Four reasons why cloud is the future of the media and entertainment industry," https://www.disguise.one/en/insights/blog/four-reasons-why-cloud-is-the-future-of-the-media-and-entertainment-industry

[3] M. N. O. Sadiku, U. C. Chukwu, and J. O. Sadiku, "Cloud computing in media & entertainment," *American Journal of Social and Humanitarian Research*, vol. 6, no. 11, November 2023, pp. 58-66.

[4] M. N. O. Sadiku, P. A. Adekunte, and J. O. Sadiku, "Cloud computing in media and entertainment," *International Journal of Trend in Scientific Research and Development*, vol. 9, no. 3, May-June 2025, pp. 795-803.

[5] S. Ezell and B. Swanson, "How cloud computing enables modern manufacturing," June 2017 https://itif.org/publications/2017/06/22/how-cloud-computing-enables-modern-manufacturing

[6] "Stay safe online: Importance of cloud application security," September 2024, https://litslink.com/blog/cloud-application-security

[7] "Features of cloud computing – 10 major characteristics of cloud computing," https://data-flair.training/blogs/features-of-cloud-computing/

[8] "Cloud manufacturing," *Wikipedia*, the free encyclopedia https://en.wikipedia.org/wiki/Cloud_manufacturing

[9] "Banking on the cloud: The role of cloud computing in modern financial services," February 2025,

https://www.neosofttech.com/blogs/cloud-computing-financial-services/

[10] "Why media and entertainment firms must become cloud-native," October 2021,

https://www.birlasoft.com/articles/why-media-entertainment-must-become-cloud-native

[11] "Conquering the media and entertainment industry with cloud computing," October 2020,

https://www.xavor.com/blog/conquering-the-media-and-entertainment-industry-with-cloud-computing/

[12] "Cloud computing in media and entertainment industry: A guide for producers and users,"

https://symphony-solutions.com/insights/cloud-computing-in-media-and-entertainment-industry

[13] J. Karlin, "How cloud computing is transforming the media and entertainment industry," September 2024,

https://acecloud.ai/resources/public-cloud/cloud-computing-in-media-entertainment/

[14] "How the cloud is revolutionising the media and entertainment industry,"

https://nexstor.com/how-the-cloud-is-revolutionising-the-media-and-entertainment-industry/

[15] "Media & entertainment industry casting call: High resolution digital assets offer new role for petabyte storage,"

https://www.smartdatacollective.com/media-entertainment-industry-casting-call-high-resolution-digital-assets-offer-n/

[16] K. Paulsen, "The challenges of cloud computing in 2025," December 2024,

https://www.tvtechnology.com/opinion/the-challenges-of-cloud-computing-in-2025

[17] J. Lafleur, "Survey says: Cloud storage makes strong gains for media & entertainment," April 2019,

https://www.backblaze.com/blog/cloud-storage-makes-strong-gains-in-media-entertainment/

CHAPTER 7
BLOCKCHAIN IN
MEDIA AND ENTERTAINMENT

"Setting an example is not the main means of influencing others; it is the only means."

— Albert Einstein

7.1 INTRODUCTION

Blockchain is a digital, decentralized method of chronologically recording transactions in real-time that was originally developed to enable the concept of cryptocurrency, specifically Bitcoin, over a decade ago. Blockchain technology is transforming media and entertainment by reducing piracy, increasing transparency, connecting artists directly with fans, and verifying scarcity of digital collectibles. It is now starting to impact numerous industries, with great potential to have a major effect on media and entertainment in the coming years [1].

The technology that was designed to be the foundation for Bitcoin is now available for use in a variety of new business applications and industries. A blockchain is essentially a digital distributed ledger. It records transactions in real time, chronologically, and immutably. From medicine to retail and economics, there is hardly any facet that blockchain has not pervaded. The television and media industry as a whole, can benefit from using blockchain technology in several ways — through advertising, distribution, and content creation and verification. Because the media and entertainment industry is vast, this technology has the potential to benefit the key stakeholders. Given its ability to store and share a unique and immutable set of records in a decentralized way, blockchain could transform content distribution, digital rights management, data storage, gaming, and advertising [2].

Blockchain is a secure, encrypted, digital distributed ledger that is chronologically time-stamped with unalterable data. It is transforming the media and entertainment industry by offering solutions for copyright protection, royalty distribution, and content creation. Blockchain technology is making a significant impact across various sectors of the entertainment industry. It has become popular in the media, advertising, and entertainment industries. The integration of Blockchain for media and entertainment marks a significant step towards improved transparency, security, and efficiency [3].

In this chapter, we will understand the potential of blockchain for media and entertainment. The chapter begins with explaining the concept of blockchain. It discusses blockchain in media and entertainment and provides some industrial examples. It covers some applications of blockchain in the media and entertainment industry. It highlights the benefits and challenges of blockchain in media and entertainment. The last section concludes with comments.

7.2 WHAT IS BLOCKCHAIN?

Blockchain, a type of distributed digital ledger technology (DLT), is a relatively new and exciting way of recording transactions in the digital age. It is a decentralized and distributed digital ledger technology that securely records and verifies transactions across multiple computers or nodes in a network. Basically, it is a chain of blocks in which each block contains a list of transactions. The symbol of a blockchain is depicted in Figure 7.1 [4].

Figure 7.1 The symbol of blockchain [4].

The blockchain technology was created as the foundational basis for Bitcoin – a digital currency in which secure peer-to-peer transactions occur over the Internet. It is expected that the spending on blockchain solutions worldwide would grow from 4.5 billion USD (2020) to an estimated value of 19 billion USD by 2024 [5].

Originally developed as the accounting method for the virtual currency Bitcoin, Blockchains are appearing in a variety of commercial applications today. Blockchain technology is a type of distributed digital ledger that uses encryption to make entries permanent and tamper-proof and can be programmed to record financial transactions. It is used for secure transfer of money, assets, and information via a computer network such as the Internet without requiring a third-party intermediary. It is now being adopted across financial and non-financial sectors. As a catalyst for change, the Blockchain technology is going to change the business world and financial matters in major ways.

The first Blockchain was conceived in 2008 by an anonymous person or group known as Satoshi Nakamoto, who published a white paper introducing the concept of a peer-to-peer electronic cash system he called Bitcoin [6,7]. Bitcoin and Ethereum are the first two mainstream blockchains. Other modern blockchains include Namecoin, Peercoin, Ether, and Litccoin. Figure 7.2 shows different components of blockchain [8].

Figure 7.2 Different components of blockchain [8].

Blockchain combines existing technologies such as distributed digital ledgers, encryption, immutable records management, asset tokenization and decentralized governance to capture and record information that participants in a network need to interact and transact. As illustrated in Figure 7.3, a complete blockchain incorporates all the following five elements [9]:

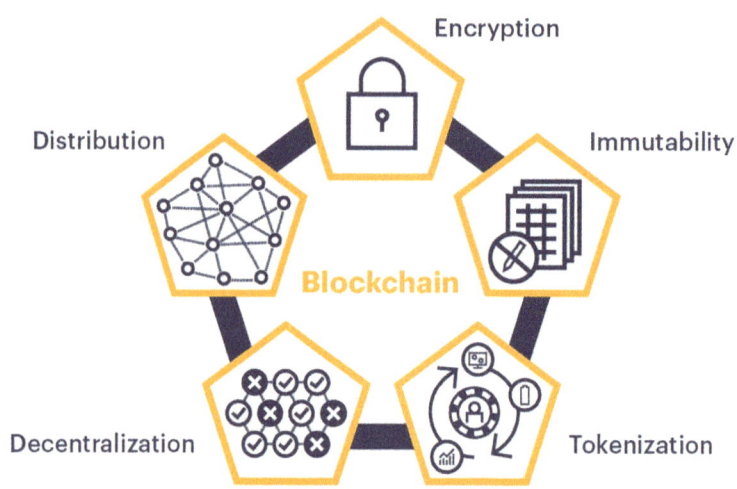

Figure 7.3 Five key elements of Blockchain [9].

- *Distribution:* Digital assets are distributed, not copied or transferred. A protocol establishes a set of rules in the form of distributed mathematical computations that ensures the integrity of the data exchanged among a large number of computing devises without going though a trusted third party. A centralized architecture presents several issues including a single point of failure and problems of scalability.

• *Encryption:* BC uses technologies such as public and private keys to record data securely and semi-anonymously. Completed transactions are cryptographically signed, time-stamped, and sequentially added to the ledger.

• *Immutability:* The blockchain was designed so these transactions are immutable, i.e. they cannot be deleted. No entity can modify the transaction records. Thus, Blockchains are secure and meddle-free by design. Data can be distributed, but not copied.

• *Tokenization:* Value is exchanged in the form of tokens, which can represent a wide variety of asset types, including monetary assets, units of data or user identities.

• *Decentralization:* No single entity controls a majority of the nodes or dictates the rules. A consensus mechanism verifies and approves transactions, eliminating the need for a central intermediary to govern the network.

Bitcoin and its underlying blockchain technology increasingly impact all facets of society. Bitcoin's status as digital gold is merely the tip of this technology. Figure 7.4 shows Bitcoin [10], while Figure 7.5 shows how blockchain works [11].

Figure 7.4 Bitcoin [10].

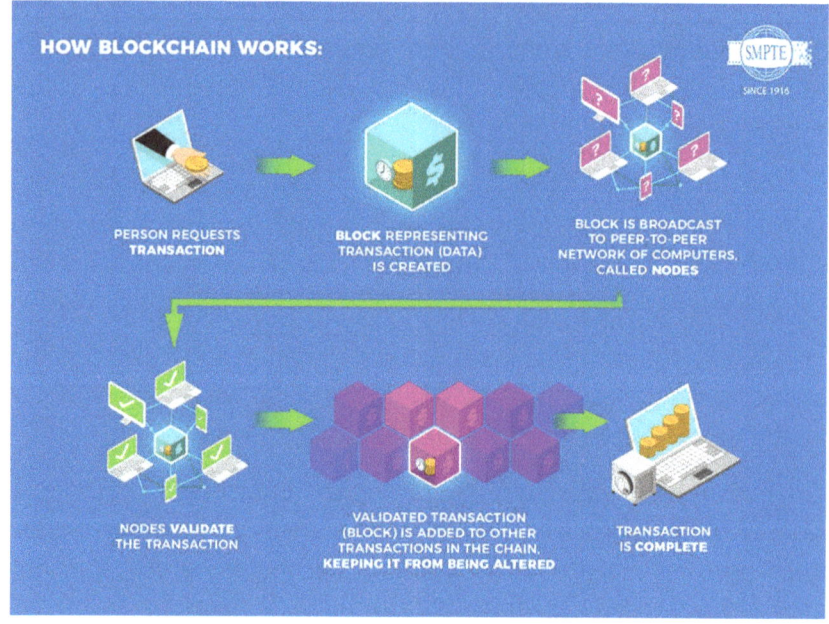

Figure 7.5 How blockchain works [11].

Although blockchain technology will for all time be associated with Bitcoin due to their common genesis, it has broader applications. Cryptocurrency will increasingly become a factor in family law issues as well.

A blockchain is a tamper-proof, distributed database that stores blocks of information for cryptographically bound transactions via peer-to-peer networks. At the heart of blockchain's functionality is cryptographic hashing. Each block in a blockchain contains a cryptographic hash of the previous block, creating an immutable chain of blocks. If anyone attempts to tamper with the data in a block, it would alter the block's hash. This would disrupt the entire chain, making it virtually impossible to manipulate. The security feature ensures data integrity and prevents unauthorized changes [12].

In a nutshell, blockchain technology involves three basic concepts [13]: (1) It is a system for recording a series of data items (such as transactions between parties); (2) It uses cryptography to make it difficult to tamper with past entries; (3) It has an agreed process for storing copies of the ledger and adding new entries (also called a consensus protocol).

Blockchain is a novel decentralized infrastructure and distributed computing paradigm that uses a chained data structure for verification, storage, and distributed consensus algorithms to generate and update data. Decentralization is a key feature of blockchain technology, which refers to the distribution of power and decision-making across a network of nodes or participants rather than being controlled by a central authority or system. It provides robustness while eliminating many-to-one traffic flows to avoid delays and single points of failure. Figure 7.6 shows the decentralized property of blockchain [11]. The advantages of decentralized property of blockchain network include the following [11]:

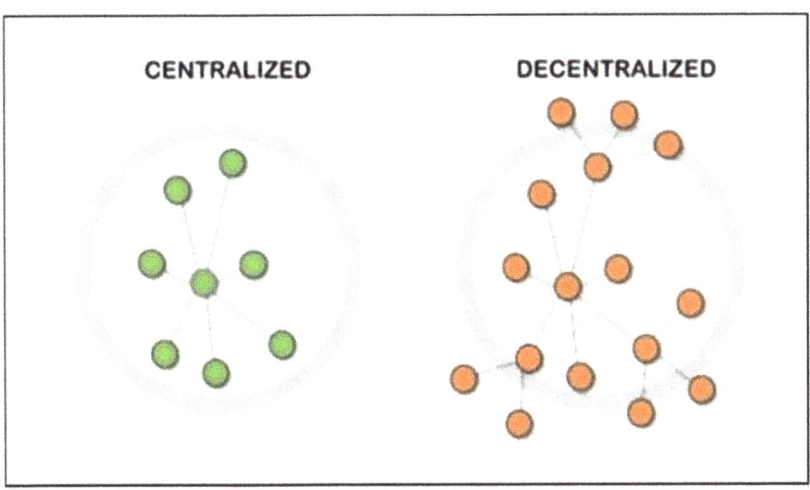

Figure 7.6 The decentralized property of blockchain [11].

- The decentralized property of blockchain makes it less prone to failure and more expensive for hackers to attack the network.

- There is no third-party involvement; therefore, there is no added risk.

- Every change made in the network is traceable and concrete.

- Users maintain full autonomy of their properties and are not dependent on third parties to maintain and manage their assets.

- It provides enhanced security.

7.3 BLOCKCHAIN IN MEDIA AND ENTERTAINMENT

The world has become a small, interconnected community. With it, demand for blockchain in media advertising and entertainment market is growing as traditional marketing quickly adopts online ad buying, web-based tagging, and other technologies. It is now employed in different areas and new business models, like buyer hardware, media and diversion, car, aviation, safeguard, material, energy, power, food and refreshments, etc. The media and entertainment sector is quickly adopting this technology as the market share for entertainment keeps expanding. Blockchain and other cutting-edge technologies are revolutionizing the media industry and the entertainment sector by enabling real-time consumption. Blockchain in media advertising and entertainment has become a key player in the advertising and entertainment market. Figure 7.7 shows a representation of the entertainment industry [14].

Figure 7.7 A representation of the entertainment industry [14].

The blockchain in the media, advertising, and entertainment market is segmented by application (licensing and rights management, digital advertising, smart contracts, online gaming, and payments), type of blockchain (public, private), size of the enterprise (small and medium enterprises, large enterprises), and geography (North America, Europe, Asia-Pacific, Latin America, and the Middle East and Africa) [15]. The technology is promising in transforming how entertainment content, e.g., films, videos, music, etc., is provided, used, and paid for. It can generally change how the creators and consumers deliver, enjoy, and pay for types of entertainment.

7.4 INDUSTRIAL EXAMPLES OF BLOCKCHAIN IN MEDIA AND ENTERTAINMENT

Many nations have gained various opportunities through advanced technologies and global media blockchain in advertising and entertainment. Large enterprises on various digital platforms highly use blockchain as an application in the advertising and entertainment market. Some implementations of blockchain in M&E industry include the following [16]:

• *Audius:* This is a blockchain-based music streaming platform that connects artists directly with their fans. It was founded in 2018 by Roneil Rumburg and Forrest Browning. The platform was launched in beta in 2019 and went live in 2020. The platform has over 250,000 artists and one million songs on its platform. Audius has raised over $50 million in funding from investors. Audius has a number of advantages over the traditional music streaming services. It eliminates intermediaries and is decentralized, which means that it is not controlled by a central authority. Listeners on Audius can earn rewards for listening to music, which gives them an incentive to support their favorite artists. Audius faces competition from major music streaming services such as Spotify and Apple Music.

• *SingularDTV:* SingularDTV uses blockchain to empower artists and content creators. It offers tools to manage intellectual property rights, royalties, and distribution in a transparent and decentralized manner. Creators can track their content's usage and receive fair compensation automatically through smart contracts.

• *Verasity:* Verasity uses blockchain to combat ad fraud and provide fair compensation to content creators. Through its Proof of View technology, it ensures that video views are genuine, preventing ad fraud, and ensuring that creators receive accurate revenue.

• *Flixxo:* This is a decentralized video sharing platform that combines blockchain and peer-to-peer technology. Content creators are rewarded with Flixx tokens based on the popularity of their content, and viewers can earn tokens by watching and sharing videos.

• *BlueSnap:* The preferred worldwide payment orchestration platform for major B2B and B2C companies announced a new collaboration with BitPay, the prominent provider of Bitcoin and cryptocurrency payment services. This product partnership helps BlueSnap reach its goal of helping businesses around the world make more money and cut costs by letting them accept and be paid in up to 15 different cryptocurrencies and seven fiat currencies.

• *Soney:* The Japanese media giant is dipping its foot into blockchain waters. Sony filed a patent for a blockchain solution to be used in user verification and storing digital rights. According to the company, current digital rights management solutions are insecure and unreliable.

7.5 APPLICATIONS OF BLOCKCHAIN IN MEDIA AND ENTERTAINMENT

Common applications of blockchain in media and entertainment include the following [17,18]:

• *Payments:* One of the most obvious applications of blockchain in the media is its ability to support micropayments that can be processed without the need for an intermediary payment network or its fees. Generally speaking, without blockchain, intermediary payment fees are too cost-prohibitive to enable micro-payments. Today, we are already seeing startups that are exploring new payment models through blockchain technology that are focused upon bringing more value to content creators. Pay-per-use consumption has become feasible due to blockchain-powered micropayments. Smart contracts, self-executing agreements powered by blockchain, play a pivotal role in automating royalty payments.

• *Tokenization of Assets:* Blockchain introduces the concept of tokenization, allowing content creators to tokenize their intellectual property. Blockchain platforms have recently announced capabilities allowing artists to tokenize their work, a process that divides a digital asset into multiple tokens. This fractional ownership model enables fans to invest in and own a share of their favorite content. The tokenization aspect of the blockchain platform heralds an era where digital assets, such as songs, movies, or art, can be tokenized as NFTs (non-fungible tokens). This not only allows artists to monetize their work in innovative ways but also provides consumers with unique, personalized ownership of digital media content.

• *Smart Contracts:* These automated, self-executing contracts handle the terms of the agreement between buyer and seller. It brings a new level of interactivity to content consumption. Blockchain-based smart contracts automate agreements and transactions, streamlining processes like content licensing and payment settlements. One major benefit of blockchain is enabling direct connections between artists and their fans or consumers, facilitated by smart contracts that can automatically enforce fair terms and facilitate micropayments. Smart contracts also empower artists with the ability to track every stream across the web and not miss out on potential royalties. Smart contracts play a pivotal role in the governance models of consortium blockchains in entertainment. These self-executing contracts are programmable agreements that automatically enforce predefined rules and conditions.

• *Disintermediation:* Traditionally, the M&E industries have been dominated by intermediaries, creating inefficiencies in content monetization, rights management, and advertising targeting. Imagine a world where your favorite musicians and artists can directly share their masterpieces with you, without having to go through big companies. This is now possible thanks to the media and entertainment industries tapping into blockchain technology. The advertising and media industry is rife with intermediaries. On-demand streaming services like YouTube, Spotify, Apple Music, and Soundcloud are intermediaries as well as industry players like recorded music companies, music publishers, music managers, and music distributors. Smart contracts automate and streamline royalty payments, ensuring artists, musicians, and other content creators get their due without significant chunks of their profits being taken by intermediaries. By enabling direct creator-audience interaction, blockchain helps democratize participation, moving control away from centralized legacy platforms. Enthusiasts, gamers, and creators can interact without costly intermediaries, ensuring that more revenue streams back to the creators themselves.

• *Online Gaming:* The gaming and eSports sectors are experiencing a blockchain-driven transformation. Blockchain technology introduces secure ownership of in-game assets, transparent tournament systems, and decentralized gaming platforms. Gamers now have true ownership of virtual assets and can participate in fair competitions. Blockchain experts can write smart contracts and deal with blockchain-based online gaming. Neither can anyone change the public location where the in-game resources are put away, nor can anyone privately supplant the responsibility for resources. They will stay the property of the game player who claims them.

7.6 BENEFITS

The benefits of blockchain in media production are remarkable. It brings an exceptional level of transparency and traceability to financial transactions, protects against piracy, and promotes direct connections between content creators and consumers. Benefits of blockchain in media advertising and entertainment market are likely to expand. Blockchain eliminates the risk of digital fraud. Other benefits of blockchain in the media and entertainment industry include the following [19]:

• *Protection of IP:* Intellectual property issues and violations are pervasive in the media and entertainment industries. Musicians, artists, and other entertainers have long struggled to maintain ownership over their work. One of the most significant challenges faced by the media industry today is piracy. Blockchain allows for time-stamping and verification of digital content, making it easier to prove ownership and combat piracy. Blockchain technology can track the lifecycle of any asset, and thereby reduce piracy of intellectual property (IP), protect digital content, and facilitate the distribution of authentic digital collectibles. Enterprise Ethereum allows artists and creators to digitize the metadata of their unique content, manage, and store IP rights on a time-stamped, immutable ledger. This means unauthorized use, distribution, or piracy of intellectual property, especially digital content, can be considerably reduced.

• *Royalty Distribution:* Blockchain can be used to track royalties for artists and creators. It can facilitate transparent and efficient royalty payments to artists, writers, and other contributors, ensuring fair compensation. Blockchain uses smart contracts to automate royalty payments based on predefined terms. This ensures content creators receive fair compensation without delays or disputes. Royalty payments can be programmed into a smart contract for every piece of content and can be automatically paid out to the creator upon usage.

• *Transparency:* Blockchain technology inherently promotes transparency. It offers noteworthy advertisement transparency and a better perspective on how media content gets consumers. Every transaction made on a blockchain platform is recorded and can be tracked in real-time. For artists, this means they can verify the usage of their digital assets and ensure they're receiving the correct royalty payments.

• *Traceability:* Blockchain enables the creation of a transparent and traceable supply chain for digital content. From the moment of creation to its distribution and consumption, every transaction is recorded on the blockchain. This ensures that content creators and rights holders can trace the journey of their intellectual property, identifying any unauthorized distribution or usage along the way.

• *New Revenue Streams:* Blockchain can boost revenue for creators since they provide value-added digital content for limited customers. Blockchain technology enables the creation of new revenue models, such as micropayments and NFTs, offering artists and creators more opportunities to connect with their audience. The rise of blockchain-based marketplaces means artists and creators can sell their work directly to consumers. This direct approach not only boosts revenue streams but allows users to interact without costly intermediaries.

• *Decentralization:* Blockchain facilitates the development of decentralized content distribution platforms that operate on a peer-to-peer network. Think of decentralizing as breaking up a big group into smaller teams. So instead of one big company controlling everything, many small groups or people share the power. This means artists do not have to share their earnings with big companies, called intermediaries. Instead, they get to keep more of what they earn. Through a myriad of blockchain use cases, artists and businesses alike are harnessing decentralized platforms to introduce transparency, eliminate intermediaries, and foster genuine connections between creators and their audience.

• *Global Collaboration:* Blockchain's global reach fosters collaboration and standardization in the content licensing space. The use of common standards and protocols on blockchain networks allows for interoperability between different platforms and ecosystems. Blockchain's decentralized system breaks down geographical barriers, enabling creators from around the world to work together easily. This global collaboration promotes diversity and sparks innovative content creation.

• *Competitive Landscape:* The competitive landscape of the global blockchain in the media, advertising, and entertainment industries is moderately concentrated, as only a few players offer blockchain solutions, especially in the media and entertainment industries.

• *Data Privacy:* Blockchain's decentralized nature contributes to enhanced data privacy in ticketing systems. Instead of storing sensitive information in a central database, personal data related to ticket transactions can be encrypted and stored in a decentralized manner. This minimizes the risk of data breaches and unauthorized access to attendees' personal information.

Some of these benefits are shown in Figure 7.8 [17].

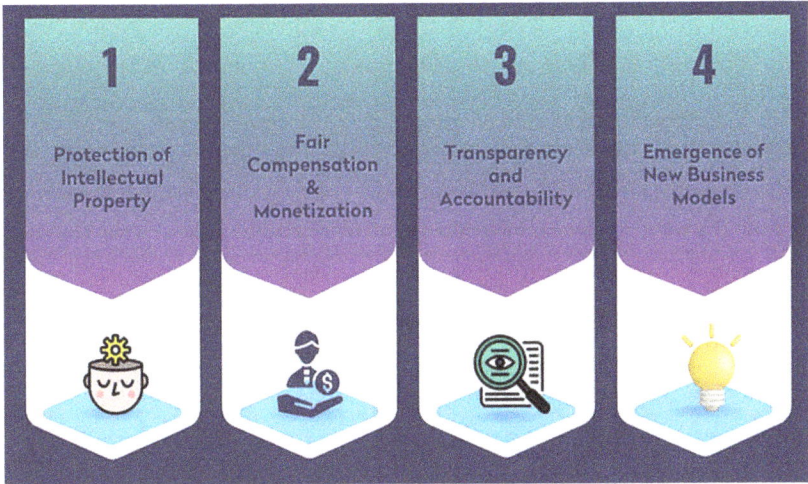

Figure 7.8 Some benefits of blockchain in media and entertainment [17].

7.7 CHALLENGES

While blockchain technology offers exciting possibilities for the entertainment industry, it also faces certain challenges and limitations. Despite the promising potential, issues such as complexity, cost, and regulation limit the evolution of this technology. Piracy is the worst challenge since it is hard to control the ownership, distribution, and identity. One major challenge is scalability. Another limitation is the lack of mainstream adoption. While blockchain-based platforms have gained traction within niche communities, they have yet to reach mainstream audiences. Blockchain is now unregulated, and normal principles for using innovation to make esteem should be made. Other challenges of blockchain in the media and entertainment industry include the following [20,21]:

• *Scalability:* One of the main challenges is the ability of blockchain networks to handle a large number of transactions, especially as the entertainment industry continues to expand rapidly. It is important to find flexible solutions to meet the increasing demands. The key challenges of scalability that once held blockchain back are now being addressed.

• *Regulatory Landscape:* Blockchain's decentralized nature can sometimes clash with existing legal frameworks and industry regulations. It is crucial to effectively address these regulatory issues and ensure compliance. The regulatory landscape surrounding blockchain in the entertainment industry is still evolving. Different jurisdictions have varying regulations and laws concerning the use of blockchain technology, which can present legal challenges for artists and creators looking to leverage blockchain platforms.

• *Technical Difficulties:* Implementing blockchain media production requires overcoming technical challenges. This includes seamlessly integrating blockchain into current systems and creating user-friendly interfaces.

• *Transparency:* Transactions on the blockchain are visible to its participants, increasing auditability and trust. IP issues in the music industry are fueled by a lack of transparency. Artists often do not fully understand the terms of contracts and copyrights, which limits their ability to ensure they are fairly compensated. All blockchain transactions are transparent and traceable. This builds trust among everyone involved in content creation and distribution, reducing disputes and improving collaboration.

• *Trust:* Trust in the media has reached all-time lows. This has been fueled by fake news, which has undermined the public's confidence in the media and left many consumers misinformed. At its core, blockchain's strength lies in its immutable and transparent characteristics. This not only enhances security, fostering more trust in the media but also catalyzes a more direct interaction between creators and consumers. Because blockchain precludes the need for a middleman, the technology creates new opportunities for large corporations to get closer to their customers and consumers.

• *Scarcity:* Generally digital objects can lose value because they are easily copied. We see this especially in the area of pirated music, movies, and TV. But because blockchain makes it possible for creators to register origin of work and set sharing permissions, structure the means of exchange that they are willing to accept, it is possible create conditions for "digital scarcity."

• *Security:* The idea of blockchain innovation permits creators to precisely and safely track the development of their blockchain-facilitated content by confirming, paying customers, and breaking down appropriation designs because of its straightforwardness. Blockchain is secure and it is near difficult to "hack" the information. Blockchain can counter piracy in several ways. It can create a secure and transparent record of digital content ownership, simplifying the process of tracking and prosecuting pirates.

• *Lack of Standardization:* Smart contracts, which automate various processes in the media supply chain, may lack standardization across different blockchain networks. This can result in compatibility issues, making it challenging to execute uniform agreements and transactions. Establishing universal standards and protocols for data representation and smart contracts is crucial for interoperability. Standardizing smart contracts or creating interoperable versions that can function seamlessly across various blockchain networks is essential.

• *Data Protection:* With the vast amounts of user data involved in media and entertainment, compliance with data protection and privacy regulations is paramount. Blockchain's transparency can be leveraged to enhance data security, but it must also adhere to stringent privacy laws such as the General Data Protection Regulation (GDPR) in Europe or similar regulations in other jurisdictions.

Some of these challenges are shown in Figure 7.9 [22].

Challenges and Limitations
of Blockchain in Entertainment

 Scalability Issues in Blockchain Implementation

 Regulatory Challenges and Compliance

 Overcoming Technical Hurdles

Figure 7.9 Some challenges of blockchain in media and entertainment [22].

7.8 CONCLUSION

As the entertainment and media industry continues its digital transformation, many are beginning to realize the potential of blockchain technology to reshape the way content is created, distributed, and consumed. The value of blockchain technology has the potential to redefine the very fabric of the entertainment world. The role of blockchain technology in the media and entertainment industries is rapidly evolving, making it an exciting time to be a part of the change. Blockchain is emerging as a critical tool in combatting fraud and enhancing transparency in digital advertising. It is disrupting not only the existing business models but is also enabling the development of new business models, especially in the media industry [23].

Blockchain technology is revolutionizing the media, advertising, and entertainment industries by offering innovative solutions for issues related to transparency, content distribution, intellectual property management, and revenue sharing. As the digital revolution surges forward, the role of blockchain technology in the media and entertainment industries is becoming increasingly significant. More information on the integration of blockchain technology into the media and entertainment industry is available from the books in [24-28] and a related journal: *IEEE Blockchain.*

REFERENCES

[1] "Blockchain in media and entertainment,"

https://www.smpte.org/blockchain

[2] C. Batista, "Blockchain might be the future of the media and entertainment industry,"

https://www.bairesdev.com/blog/blockchain-might-be-the-future-of-the-media/

[3] M. N. O. Sadiku, P. A. Adekunte, and J. O. Sadiku, "Blockchain in media and entertainment," *International Journal of Trend in Scientific Research and Development*, vol. 9, no. 3, May-June 2025, pp. 410-420.

[4] "Exploring the impact of blockchain in media and entertainment,"

https://mitechnews.com/guest-columns/exploring-the-impact-of-blockchain-in-media-and-entertainment/

[5] C. M. M. Kotteti and M. N. O. Sadiku, "Blockchain technology," *International Journal of Trend in Research and Development*, vol. 10, no. 3, May-June 2023, pp. 274-276.

[6] "Blockchain," *Wikipedia*, the free encyclopedia

https://en.wikipedia.org/wiki/Blockchain

[7] S. Nakamoto, "Bitcoin: A peer-to-peer electronic cash system,"

https://bitcoin.org/bitcoin.pdf

[8] "The beginning of a new era in technology: Blockchain traceability,"

https://www.visiott.com/blog/blockchain-traceability/#:~:text=The%20Beginning%20of%20a%20New,money%20without%20a%20central%20bank.

[9] "The CIO's guide to blockchain,"

https://www.gartner.com/smarterwithgartner/the-cios-guide-to-blockchain#:~:text=True%20blockchain%20has%20five%20elements,%2C%20immutability%2C%20tokenization%20and%20decentralization.

[10] "Blockchain and space exploration: Is decentralized data the future of space missions?" October 2024,

https://medium.com/coinmonks/is-decentralized-data-the-future-of-space-missions-646173d1aeec

[11] E. Fiorino, "Could blockchain be a game changer for media and entertainment?" September 2019,

https://www.smpte.org/blog/could-blockchain-be-game-changer-media-and-entertainment

[12] D. Singh, "Blockchain in pharmaceutical supply chain: The next big frontier," October 2023,

https://www.debutinfotech.com/blog/blockchain-in-pharmaceutical-supply-chain-the-next-big-frontier

[13] D. Michels, "Technology blockchain and telecoms,"

https://www.iicom.org/wp-content/uploads/22-26-blockchain.pdf

[14] "How does blockchain change the entertainment industry?" October 2022,

https://cystack.net/blog/blockchain-entertainment-industry

[15] "Blockchain in media and entertainment market size & share analysis - Growth trends & forecasts (2025 - 2030),"

https://www.mordorintelligence.com/industry-reports/blockchain-in-media-advertising-and-entertainment-market

[16] "Blockchain for media production: Redefining media creation," February 2025,

https://webisoft.com/articles/blockchain-for-media-production/

[17] "Blockchain in media and entertainment," August 2023,

https://medium.com/blockchain-hacks/blockchain-in-media-and-entertainment-86e36e9ca34a

[18] V. Panday, "How blockchain is shaping the future of entertainment and media,"

https://www.linkedin.com/pulse/how-blockchain-shaping-future-entertainment-media-dr-vivek-pandey-rhfzf/

[19] "Blockchain in media & entertainment,"

https://consensys.io/blockchain-use-cases/media-and-entertainment

[20] F. Fatemi, "Blockchain technology solves some of the biggest key challenges faced by media and entertainment companies," May 2022,

https://www.forbes.com/sites/falonfatemi/2022/05/06/blockchain-technology-solves-some-of-the-biggest-key-challenges-faced-by-media-and-entertainment-companies/

[21] J. Sticca, "How blockchain will transform media and entertainment,"

https://www.trueinteraction.com/how-blockchain-will-transform-media-and-entertainment/

[22] "Blockchain for media production: Redefining media creation,"

https://webisoft.com/articles/blockchain-for-media-production/

[23] "How does blockchain change the entertainment industry?" October 2022,

https://cystack.net/blog/blockchain-entertainment-industry

[24] M. N. O. Sadiku, *Blockchain Technology and Its Applications*. Moldova, Europe: Lambert Academic Publishing, 2023.

[25] P. M. Parker, *The 2023 Report on Blockchain in Media, Advertising, and Entertainment: World Market Segmentation by City*. ICON Group International, 2022.

[26] P. Poujol, *Online Film Production in China Using Blockchain and Smart Contracts (International Series on Computer, Entertainment and Media Technology)*. Springer, 2019.

[27] P. M. Parker, *The 2025-2030 World Outlook for Blockchain in Media, Advertising, and Entertainment*. ICON Group International, 2024.

[28] G. Blokdyk, *Blockchain in Media and Entertainment. 5STARCooks*, 2nd edition, 2018.

CHAPTER 8
IMMERSIVE TECHNOLOGIES IN MEDIA AND ENTERTAINMENT

"You build on failure. You use it as a stepping stone. Close the door on the past. You don't try to forget the mistake, but you don't dwell on it. You don't let it have any of your energy, or any of your time, or any of your space."

— Johnny Cash

8.1 INTRODUCTION

The entertainment industry has been directly influenced by technological advancement since time immemorial. Right from the advent of television, popularity of the Internet, to the current technological landscape of several disruptive technologies, the entertainment industry has been directly impacted.

Immersive technology aims to transport users to virtual environments or enhance their real-world experiences by overlaying digital information onto their physical surroundings. By leveraging cutting-edge hardware and software, immersive technology creates a truly captivating experience that engages all your senses. Based on technology, the immersive entertainment market is segmented into virtual reality (VR), augmented reality (AR), mixed reality (XR), and others. The immersive experience has been fueled by technological advancements such as virtual reality (VR) and augmented reality (AR), which have also expedited the entertainment industry's rapid expansion. VR and AR are being used to create immersive cinematic experiences, allowing viewers to explore narratives from different perspectives and interact with the story. AR can be used to enhance live events, such as concerts or sporting events, by adding digital elements to the viewing experience. Figure 8.1 shows a typical entertainment live event [1].

Figure 8.1 A typical entertainment live event [1].

Immersive technology refers to any technology that blurs the line between the physical and digital worlds, creating a sense of presence and engagement for the user. It can be broadly categorized into three main types: virtual reality (VR), augmented reality (AR), and mixed reality (MR). Immersive technologies are revolutionizing the media and entertainment industry by creating highly engaging and interactive experiences [2].

This chapter examines the integration of immersive technology in the media and entertainment industry. It begins with explaining immersive technologies. It describes immersive technologies in the media and entertainment industry and provides some applications. It highlights the benefits and challenges of immersive technologies in media and entertainment. The last section concludes with comments.

8.2 WHAT ARE IMMERSIVE TECHNOLOGIES?

The first step in understanding how to use immersive technologies is to learn the differences between various forms. In their simplest form, immersive technologies consist in adding virtual objects to the real world. There are four types of digital realities leading to different types of immersive technologies [3,4]:

- *Augmented reality* (AR)— designed to add digital elements over real-world views with limited interaction.

- *Virtual reality* (VR)— immersive experiences helping to isolate users from the real world, usually via a headset device and headphones designed for such activities.

- *Mixed reality* (MR)— combining AR and VR elements so that digital objects can interact with the real world means businesses can design elements anchored within a real environment.

- *Extended reality* (XR)— covering all types of technologies that enhance our senses, including the three types previously mentioned.

These devices also enable new user interactions including spatially tracked 3D controllers, voice inputs, gaze tracking, and hand gesture controls.

Extended reality (XR) is the overarching term used to describe employing technology to blend real life and the digital world. It includes all the machine-human interfaces beyond the physical realm (reality) such as augmented reality (AR), mixed reality (MR), assisted reality (aR), and virtual reality (VR), as illustrated in Figure 8.2 [5]. Figure 8.3 shows the XR spectrum [6].

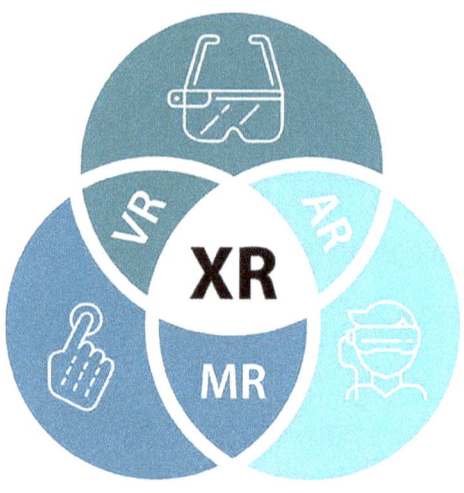

Figure 8.2 Extended reality (XR) includes AR, MR, and VR [5].

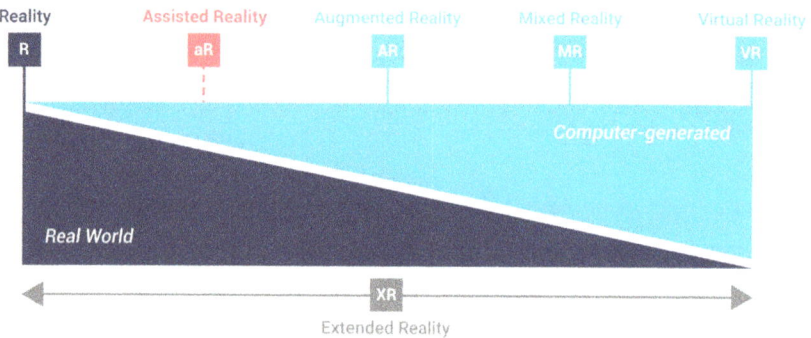

Figure 8.3 The XR spectrum [6].

Immersive technologies reside along a continuous scale ranging between the completely real and the completely virtual world. At one end, the real environment refers to the actual physical space, objects, and people that exist in the tangible world around us. At the other end, the virtual environment represents a completely computer-generated and immersive digital space, distinct from the physical reality. The space in the middle is called mixed reality, which is a blend of the real and virtual environments, where digital and physical elements coexist and interact in real time. A range of devices makes up XR, and these are used by consumers and in many industries for entertainment, safety, training, or productivity purposes.

1. *VIRTUAL REALITY:* Virtual reality (VR) is XR at its most extreme. It completely immerses the user in a digital world, often using a computer-generated environment with scenes and objects that appear to be real. The term "virtual reality" essentially means "near-reality." Virtual reality is the key technology for experiencing sensations of sight, hearing, and touch of the past, present, and future. VR is a fully immersive technology where users wear a head-mounted display and experience a simulated world of imagery and sounds. VR enables active learning. The terms, "virtual reality" and "cyberspace" are often used interchangeably. A cyberspace may be regarded as a networked virtual reality. A person using virtual reality can look around an artificial world, move around it, and interact with virtual features or items. This effect is commonly created by virtual reality headsets. Head-mounted displays immerse the user in a virtual environment. Virtual reality is a simulated experience that can be similar to or different from the real world. It is a computer-generated, 3D environment that completely immerses the senses of sight, sound, and touch. The complete immersion of the senses overwhelms users engrossing them in the action. Virtual reality technology includes multiple components divided into two main groups: hardware and software components [7].

- *Hardware Components:* The hardware components include a computer workstation, sensory displays, a tracking system, wearable devices, and input devices. Sensory displays are used to display the simulated virtual worlds to the user. The most common type is the head-mounted displays (HMDs), which is used in combination with tracking systems. Head-mounted displays are shown in Figure 8.4 [8].

Figure 8.4 Head-mounted displays [8].

Users interact with the simulated environment through some wearable devices. VR depends on special responses such as raising hands, turning the head, or swinging the body. A wearable device is important in making these effects realistic. Special input devices are required to interact with the virtual world. These include the 3D mouse, the wired glove, motion controllers, and optical tracking sensors. These devices are used to stimulate our senses together to create the illusion of reality.

- *Software Components:* Besides the hardware, the underlying software plays an important role. It is responsible for the managing of I/O devices and time-critical applications. The software components are 3D modeling software, 2D graphics software, digital sound editing software, and VR simulation software. VR technology has been designed to ensure visual comfort and ergonomic usage.

2. *AUGMENTED REALITY:* Augmented reality (AR) is a technology that combines real-world environments with computer-generated generated information such as images, text, videos, animations, and sound. It can record and analyze the

environment in real-time. In augmented reality, the user typically experiences the real world through a device such as a smartphone, tablet, smart glasses, or head-mounted display. For example, AR allows consumers to visualize a product in more detail before they purchase it. This feature enhances consumer interaction and helps them never to repurchase the wrong item. The key objective of AR is to bring computer-generated objects into the real world and allows the user only to see them. In other words, we use AR to track the position and orientation of the user's head to enhance/ augment their perception of the world. Augmented reality falls into two categories: 2D information overlays and 3D presentations, like those used with games. AR blends the virtual and real worlds by overlaying digital objects and information onto the users' view of the physical world.

To obtain a sufficiently accurate representation of reality, AR needs the following five components [8]:

- *Sensors:* AR needs suitable sensors in the environment and possibly on a user, including fine-grained geolocation and image recognition. These are activating elements that trigger the display of virtual information.

- *Image augmentation:* This requires techniques such as image processing and face recognition.

- Head-mounted Display: HMDs are used to view the augmented world where the virtual computer-generated information is properly aligned with the real world. Display technologies are of two types: video display and optical see-through display.

- *User Interface:* This includes technologies for input modalities that include gaze tracking, touch, and gesture. AR is a user interface technology in which a camera-recorded view of the real world is augmented with computer-generated content such as graphics, animations, and 2D or 3D models.

- *Information infrastructure:* AR requires significant computing and communications infrastructure undergirding all these technologies. The infrastructure determines what real-world components to augment, with what, and when.

3.   MIXED REALITY: Mixed reality (MR) is a term used to describe the merging of a real-world environment and a computer-generated one. Physical and virtual objects may co-exist in mixed reality environments and interact in real time. This is an extension of AR that allows real and virtual elements to interact in an environment. MR liberates us from screen-bound experiences by offering instinctual interactions with data in our living spaces and with our friends. Online explorers, in hundreds of millions around the world, have experienced mixed reality through their handheld devices. Mixed reality is a blend of physical and digital worlds, unlocking natural and intuitive 3D human, computer, and environmental interactions, as shown in Figure 8.5 [10] and Figure 8.6 [11].

Figure 8.5 Mixed reality is a blend of physical and digital worlds [10].

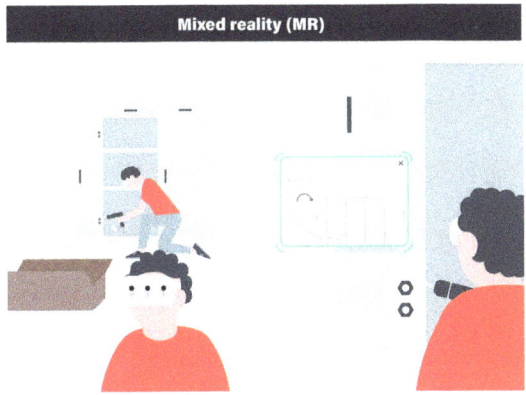

Figure 8.6 Mixed reality [11].

This new reality is based on advancements in computer vision, graphical processing, display technologies, input systems, and cloud computing. Mixed reality has been used in applications across fields including design, education, entertainment, military training, healthcare, product content management, and human-in-the-loop operation of robots [12].

4.   *ASSISTED REALITY:* Like mixed reality, assisted reality (aR) is an extension of augmented reality, with a few notable differences to both. One of these differences is that aR is primarily hands-free through the wearing of a headset, whereas AR usually requires the holding of a device such as a mobile phone. While MR is a digital-first, real-world second reality, aR is a real-world first system. It combines software and a head-mounted display. It is best experienced using smart glasses or other wearable technology. The aR market is growing rapidly and promises to be the next great leap to boost workers' productivity. A worker wearing an aR device is shown in Figure 8.7 [13].

Figure 8.7 A worker wearing an assisted reality device [13].

5. *EXTENDED REALITY:* The term "extended reality" (XR) has recently gained favor as an umbrella term that encompasses all of AR, VR, and MR. The primary user inputs for XR devices are described as follows. Voice interfaces are now ubiquitous thanks to mobile devices and standalone smart speakers. Apple's Siri, Amazon's Alexa, Google's Assistant, and Microsoft's Cortana are all voice-driven software interfaces that are continuously gaining new capabilities. Many XR devices enable user control with handheld controllers, which have capabilities beyond button press inputs. Both voice-driven interfaces and human-computer interactions have been developed specifically for XR devices, including gaze and gesture controls [14]. Figure 8.8 compares conventional computing with extended reality [14].

Conventional Computing   Extended Reality (XR)

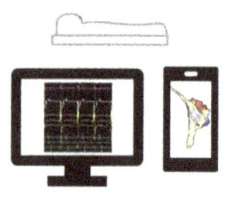
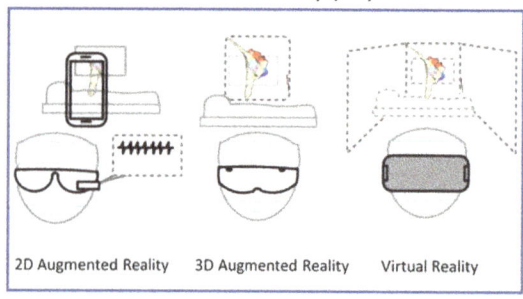

Figure 8.8 Comparing conventional computing with extended reality [14].

8.3 IMMERSIVE TECHNOLOGIES IN MEDIA AND ENTERTAINMENT

Immersive technology has become a buzzword in recent years, promising to revolutionize various industries and transform the way we experience the world around us. The concept of immersive technology has its roots in early attempts to create virtual environments for flight simulations and military training. However, the technology has come a long way since then. In terms of end user, the immersive entertainment market is segmented into media and entertainment, gaming, design and architecture, retail, education, and others. Whether it is enhancing educational experiences, improving healthcare outcomes, or revolutionizing the entertainment industry, immersive technologies are poised to redefine the way we interact with and experience the digital world [15].

8.4 APPLICATIONS OF IMMERSIVE TECHNOLOGIES IN MEDIA & ENTERTAINMENT

The potential applications of immersive technology in media and entertainment are vast and diverse. Common applications of immersive technology in media and entertainment include the following [1,16]:

• *Immersive Media:* Immersive media refers to digital technology that creates or enhances an environment, either to simulate the physical world or to create something completely new. This type of media offers a more intense and interactive experience than traditional media and engages users on various sensory levels. Immersive media and traditional media differ in some ways. Traditional media includes television, radio, newspapers, and standard non-interactive films and videos. The audience is typically a passive consumer of the content, with no control over the narrative or environment. Immersive media is characterized by its interactive nature. Users can actively participate and influence the experience. Thus, immersive media offers a more interactive, engaging, and multi-sensory experience compared to traditional media, which is generally more passive and limited in sensory engagement.

• *Immersive Entertainment:* This is about spellbinding experiences driven by cutting-edge technology that engage the senses and transport the user to a different world. Immersive entertainment has been growing steadily for the last several years, with the emergence of new venues, new business models, and a burst of creativity. Immersive experiences attempt to engage all five senses in unique physical spaces. They are evolving, offering significant growth opportunities. Immersive entertainment is quickly becoming a popular consumer segment, attracting both entrepreneurs and investors. Interactivity is a key feature of many immersive art experiences. Immersive art experiences rely on digital content, including 3D animation, motion graphics, and interactive visuals. Its market has grown significantly since its beginnings as a handful of landmark exhibitions in the early 2000s. The immersive entertainment market is worth billions and growing fast. The growth in immersive entertainment is driving interest across venue types. Casinos, hotels and resorts, retail, and even stadiums are exploring ways to tap into the trend. Figure 8.9 shows an example of immersive entertainment [17].

Figure 8.9 An example of immersive entertainment [17].

• *Interactive Media:* This can include a range of media types that respond to user input, such as video games, interactive storytelling, or educational software. Platforms like Oculus Story Studio and the National Film Board of Canada have produced interactive documentaries where viewers can engage with the content in a non-linear fashion, often impacting the narrative based on their choices. Interactions that mimic real-world behavior are intuitive and thus, the most user-friendly.

• *Immersive Audio:* Instead of superimposing visual content onto the user's environment, immersive audio overlays digital audio onto the physical soundscape. Through spatial audio technology, sounds can be positioned within a three-dimensional space for a highly immersive auditory experience. Immersive audio typically requires a device capable of delivering spatial audio, such as specialized headphones or earbuds. It may also rely on head tracking and other sensors, to adjust the experience based on a user's movements. For individuals with visual impairments, immersive audio can provide spatial cues about their environment, aiding in navigation and interaction with surroundings.

• *Gaming:* VR and AR are revolutionizing gaming by allowing for more realistic and interactive experiences. Games that require live dealers are also gaining popularity, as people appreciate the opportunity to enjoy a casino experience from home, safely and without the risk of social stigma often associated with gambling. In the gaming and entertainment sectors, immersive technologies have redefined the boundaries of user engagement, captivating audiences, and offering truly extraordinary experiences. Interactive media blurs the lines between traditional storytelling and gaming, empowering audiences to participate actively in shaping the narrative's outcome. People spend more time and money not only on video games but also on social networks, cinema, music concerts, sports games, amusement parks, etc. The market of VR games for kids is underdeveloped. Mobile gaming has particularly benefited from AR due to the ubiquity and increasing power of smartphones. Figure 8.10 shows a typical gaming [18].

Figure 8.10 A typical gaming [18].

• *Movies:* Immersive technologies can be used to create new cinematic experiences, such as interactive movies or films that spill out of the screen. VR cinema is basically filmmaking adapted to the VR medium. This novelty art form promises new and better ways of experiencing stories due to interactivity, non-linearity, and increased empathetic power. VR creates a greater sense of "presence" than traditional movie theaters or streaming services, allowing viewers to explore the movie's settings, experience the protagonist's journey, and even get involved in the action. Cinematic VR requires new forms of movie storytelling and workflows. The adoption of VR in the film industry will largely depend on the quality of storytellers and producers it attracts. The first VR movies are going to be quite costly to create, but the development can eventually lead to cheaper film production.

• *Music:* Competition drives musicians and producers to endless experimentation to stay up-to-date and relevant for the audience. The application of VR in music projects may help with both. Immersive audio technologies can create a more realistic and engaging listening experience, while AR can be used to create interactive music experiences. Major music events, such as Coachella, Lollapalooza, Sziget, or Tomorrowland, have also experimented with VR applications and 360-degree videos. AR apps can enhance live performances with immersive stories behind the music. Figure 8.11 shows a typical live music concert [19].

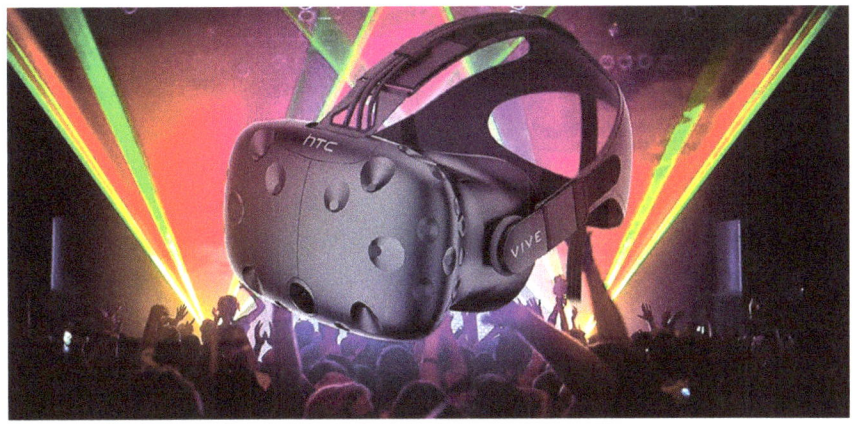

Figure 8.11 A typical live music concert [19].

• *Entertainment Parks:* Immersive rides and attractions are becoming increasingly popular, offering guests a more engaging and interactive experience. VR amusement parks are projected to offer unusual experience, entertainment, and exciting sensations to the users. Figure 8.12 shows an example of an amusement park [19].

Figure 8.12 An amusement park [19].

8.5 BENEFITS

Immersive technologies offer significant benefits to the media and entertainment industry, enhancing audience engagement, storytelling, and overall experiences. One of the primary benefits of immersive technologies is their ability to enhance user experiences. AR seamlessly blends digital information with the physical world, providing users with additional context and insights without completely detaching them from their surroundings. The primary benefit of introducing VR/AR into broadcasting and streaming is its ability to give viewers an incredibly realistic, immersive experience. Immersive technologies allow for more interactive and personalized content, pushing the boundaries of traditional media and entertainment formats. Other benefits of immersive technology in media and entertainment include the following [20]:

• *Personalization:* AR and VR allow for highly personalized content delivery, tailoring experiences to individual user preferences and behaviors. This can range from customized story paths to interactive environments that respond uniquely to each user. Personalizing experiences is also a burgeoning trend. It is no secret that people engage more when content is curated to them. Experiences can truly be unique and personalized for every visitor if supported by a clear and transparent data-capture infrastructure. Personalization leads to deeper engagement, increased opportunity for upselling and return visits, and ultimately greater brand loyalty. The use of virtual reality in entertainment adds a new dimension to traditional forms of amusement and allows more personalized experiences.

• *Life-cycle Marketing:* Attending an immersive experience is the main event, but marketing and monetization efforts are shifting to a pre-and-post model. Following attendance, providers are increasingly building longer-term relationships to drive repeat visits and merchandise sales.

• *Social Amplification:* Experiences are now preferred over products by a large portion of consumers. Crafting unique "social moments" into the experiences allows visitors to share their excitement and drive across social media. This earned social promotion can be a great marketing lever to amplify awareness.

•   *Package and Scale:* An immersive entertainment "hit" in NYC can be packaged and scaled to cities across the country and around the world. All of the launches are pursuing some versions of this model. This could be a tremendous opportunity for casinos and hotels to distinguish their properties with immersive entertainment that is localized to each property but designed on the same creative and immersive technology foundation.

•   *Enhanced Audience Engagement:* Immersive experiences create a sense of presence, allowing audiences to feel like they are actually part of the story or event. This increased engagement leads to deeper emotional connections and more memorable experiences.

•   *Improved Storytelling:* AR and VR enable new forms of storytelling, allowing for interactive and dynamic narratives where audiences can actively participate and influence the story. This can lead to more personalized and engaging experiences.

•   *Increased Interactivity:* Immersive technologies allow users to interact with digital content in a more natural way, enhancing the sense of realism and engagement. This interactivity can be applied to various forms of media, from games and movies to concerts and live events.

•   *Expanded Reach and Engagement:* Immersive technologies, especially AR and VR, can expand the reach of media and entertainment to global audiences through virtual events and experiences.

•   *Enhanced Training and Education:* Immersive experiences can be used for training and education, providing realistic simulations and interactive learning environments.

8.6 CHALLENGES

Alongside the exciting possibilities, immersive technology also presents challenges and ethical considerations that need to be addressed. As immersive technologies are relatively new, there are technical limitations and compatibility issues that content creators must navigate. Not everyone has access to the necessary hardware or software to experience immersive technologies. The industry must address challenges such as high production costs, technical constraints, and content quality to harness the full potential of these technologies. Other challenges of immersive technologies in media and entertainment include the following [21]:

• *Ethical Considerations:* Immersive technologies may collect user data during experiences, raising concerns about data privacy and security. The use of interactive media and immersive technologies may raise copyright and intellectual property issues. As immersive technology becomes more ingrained in our daily lives, ethical considerations arise surrounding privacy, data security, addiction, and the blurring of virtual and real-world boundaries. Striking the right balance between innovation and user safety will be crucial in the future.

• *Diversity and Inclusion:* Diversity and inclusion are essential elements for its evolution and relevance in today's global society. Embracing diversity means recognizing and celebrating the myriad of voices, cultures, and perspectives that make up our world. Inclusion goes beyond mere representation, fostering an environment where everyone feels valued, respected, and empowered to contribute their unique talents and experiences. When the entertainment industry embraces diversity and inclusion, it not only reflects the richness of human experiences but also resonates more deeply with audiences worldwide.

• *Safety:* Both physical safety and ethical implications are crucial for immersive media. Designers must consider user privacy, the psychological impact of immersive environments and other factors.

• *Comfort:* Designers should address physical comfort and safety, particularly for devices worn for extended periods. This includes considerations of weight, balance, and adjustable fittings. Early virtual reality systems were bulky and expensive, making them inaccessible to most consumers. However, in recent years, immersive technology has gained popularity among consumers, with VR headsets becoming more affordable and accessible. Designers must ensure that immersive experiences cater to a broad range of abilities

• *Motion Sickness:* VR, with its complete isolation from the physical world, can sometimes lead to disorientation or motion sickness for some users. Some users may experience motion sickness or other discomfort when using VR and AR devices.

• *Cost:* Creating immersive content requires significant investments in technology, talent, and production, posing financial challenges for content creators. VR and AR hardware can be expensive, making it a barrier for some consumers and businesses.

• *Content Quality:* While immersive technologies offer novel experiences, ensuring high-quality content and compelling storytelling remains crucial for long-term audience engagement.

8.7 CONCLUSION

The entertainment industry is undergoing a revolutionary transformation with the advent of immersive technologies and interactive media. Immersive technology has also made its mark in the entertainment industry, enabling users to become fully immersed in virtual worlds or interact with fictional characters and stories in new and exciting ways. From virtual reality (VR) experiences to interactive storytelling, immersive technologies have the potential to redefine entertainment. Technological advancements are expected to make immersive experiences more realistic and accessible. By embracing the transformative power of augmented reality (AR), virtual reality (VR), and mixed reality (MR), organizations will unlock unprecedented levels of engagement, efficiency, and innovation. As we look to the future, it is clear that immersive technologies will play a pivotal role

in shaping media and entertainment. More information about immersive technologies in the M&E industry can be found in the books in [22,23]

REFERENCES

[1] " N. Makarevych, "How is VR changing the entertainment and film industry?"

https://onix-systems.com/blog/virtual-reality-in-entertainment

[2] M. N. O. Sadiku, P. A. Adekunte, and J. O. Sadiku, "Immersive technologies in media and entertainment," *International Journal of Trend in Scientific Research and Development*, vol. 9, no. 3, May-June 2025, pp. 893-904.

[3] M. N. O. Sadiku, C. M. M. Kotteti, and S. M. Musa, "Augmented reality: A primer," *International Journal of Trend in Research and Development*, vol. 7, no. 3, 2020.

[4] "What is augmented reality or AR?"

https://dynamics.microsoft.com/en-us/mixed-reality/guides/what-is-augmented-reality-ar/

[5] L. van Heerden, "What is extended reality?" August 2021,

https://journeyapps.com/blog/what-is-extended-reality/

[6] A. Xperteye, "What is assisted reality? Here is what you need to know," March 2022,

https://blog.amaxperteye.com/what-is-assisted-reality-here-is-what-you-need-to-know

[7] M. O. Onyesolu and F. U. Eze, "Understanding virtual reality technology: Advances and applications," *Advances in Computer Science and Engineering*, March 2011, pp. 53-70.

[8] "Exploring the future of immersive technology," July 2023,

https://www.talespin.com/reading/exploring-the-future-of-immersive-technology

[9] M. Singh and M. P. Singh, "Augmented reality interfaces," *IEEE Internet Computing*, November/December 2013, pp. 66-70.

[10] "What is mixed reality?" January 2023,

https://learn.microsoft.com/en-us/windows/mixed-reality/discover/mixed-reality

[11] C. Rincon and J. Perez, "What are immersive technologies?" March 2025,

https://www.adalovelaceinstitute.org/resource/immersive-technologies-explainer/

[12] "Mixed reality," *Wikipedia*, the free encyclopedia,

https://en.wikipedia.org/wiki/Mixed_reality

[13] "What is assisted reality? Here is what you need to know," March 2022,

https://blog.amaxperteye.com/what-is-assisted-reality-here-is-what-you-need-to-know

[14] C. Andrews et al., "Extended reality in medical practice," *Current Treat Options Cardiovasc Medicine*, vol. 21, no. 4, March 2019.

[15] "Immersive entertainment market skyrockets to $519.77 billion by 2031 dominated by tech giants - Microsoft Corp, Qualcomm Inc and Google LLC | The Insight Partners," November 2024,

https://www.prnewswire.com/news-releases/immersive-entertainment-market-skyrockets-to-519-77-billion-by-2031-dominated-by-tech-giants---microsoft-corp-qualcomm-inc-and-google-llc--the-insight-partners-302318361.html

[16] M. Knott and M. MacLaren, "Understanding immersive entertainment," December 2024,

https://www.rolandberger.com/en/Insights/Publications/Understanding-immersive-entertainment.html

[17] "What do technology-rich immersive experiences look?"

https://www.electrosonic.com/blog/what-do-technology-rich-immersive-experiences-look-like-in-2022

[18] S. Field, "Augmented reality in entertainment & media," May 2025,

https://rockpaperreality.com/insights/ar-use-cases/augmented-reality-in-entertainment-media/

[19] L. Voutik, "How is VR one of the best technologies for the media and entertainment industry?" June 2022,

https://www.quytech.com/blog/virtual-reality-for-the-entertainment/

[20] "Entertainment trends: Immersive experiences," August 2021,

https://dimin.com/insights/entertainment-trends-immersive-experiences

[21] "Immersive media,"

https://www.interaction-design.org/literature/topics/immersive-media#:~:text=Immersive%20media%20refers%20to%20digital,users%20on%20various%20sensory%20levels.

[22] J. Dalton, *Reality Check: How Immersive Technologies Can Transform Your Business*. Kogan Page, 2021.

[23] K. Williams and M. Mascioni, *The Out-of-Home Immersive Entertainment Frontier: Expanding Interactive Boundaries in Leisure Facilities*. Routledge, 2017.

CHAPTER 9
5G NETWORK IN
MEDIA AND ENTERTAINMENT

"The world is a stage, the stage is a world of entertainment."

— Howard Dietz

9.1 INTRODUCTION

Delivering digital media, entertainment, and advertising material have historically been problematic due to technical limitations, such as slow and unreliable networks. In today's competitive market, virtualized production environments, AI-generated imaging, remote streaming connectivity, and other advanced digital technologies are key enablers for media and entertainment providers. The entertainment industry has always been one of the quickest industries to adopt the latest technologies with 5G being no exception. This technology has the potential to transform the way content is created and consumed [1]. 5G can bring fundamental changes to the entertainment broadcasting industry. The advent of 5G is certain to further the already developing entanglement between technology and entertainment companies.

5G network shows great promise in solving several issues on both the production and consumption end of media and entertainment. 5G promises, among other things, data speeds 100 times faster than 4G, 10 times lower latency, 100 times more network capacity and significantly more reliable connections. Faster download speeds and lower latency will produce high-quality, interactive video experiences without any form of interference. Figure 9.1 shows the symbol of 5G [2], while Figure 9.2 shows how 5G will impact industries [3].

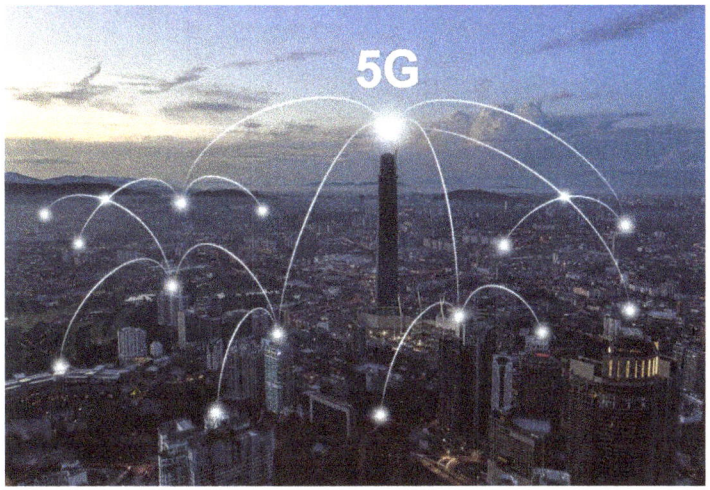

Figure 9.1 The symbol of 5G [2].

Figure 9.2 How 5G will impact industries [3].

5G is the promise of a tetherless world. It often tops the list of the many up-and-coming technologies discussed today. Innovators and technologists are investigating its potential across numerous industries, and one of the most prominent industries to come up is the media and entertainment industry. 5G technology is set to revolutionize the media and entertainment industry by enabling faster data transfer speeds and lower latency, leading to enhanced streaming quality, immersive experiences, and new content creation possibilities. As media and entertainment businesses explore 5G's potential, they are focusing on promising use cases in four areas: immersive and interactive media, streaming, live and remote productions. By unleashing the power of private 5G networks, media and entertainment studios can leverage the agility, speed, and security needed to ride the next wave of cutting-edge use cases [4].

This chapter explores several applications of 5G in the media and entertainment industry. It begins with providing an overview of 5G network. It explains 5G network in the media and entertainment industry and gives some applications. It highlights the benefits and challenges of 5G network in media and entertainment. The last section concludes with comments.

9.2 OVERVIEW OF 5G NETWORK

5G is the fifth-generation wireless cellular technology that will provide faster and more reliable communication with low latency. Compared to its predecessor, it is estimated that the 5G mobile network allows 1,000 times more data transmission compared to 4G. Like its predecessors—3G, 4G, and 4G —5G utilizes radio waves to transmit data.

Evolution from 1G to 5G is depicted in Figure 9.3 [5], while the relationship between 3G, 4G, and 5G is portrayed in Figure 9.4 [6].

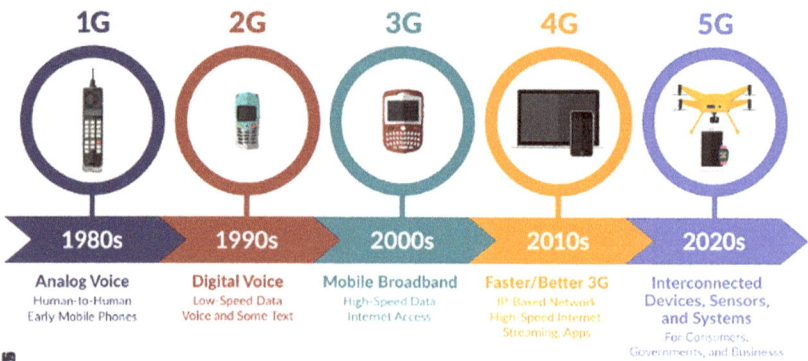

Figure 9.3 Evolution from 1G to 5G [5].

Figure 9.4 Relationship between 3G, 4G, and 5G [6].

Like any other cellular network, 5G networks send data through radio waves and operate on a cellular infrastructure, where geographic regions are partitioned into cells, each supported by an antenna and a base station. Each cell is connected to a network backbone through a wired or wireless connection. 5G may transmit data over the unlicensed frequencies currently used for Wi-Fi. It promises a smarter, faster, and more efficient network. The goal of 5G is to have far higher speeds available, at higher capacity per sector, and at far lower latency than 4G. To increase network efficiency, the cell is subdivided into micro and pico cells [7]. 5G will be a new mobile revolution as it is expected to provide gigabit-per-second data rates anytime, anywhere. 5G uses towers, as typically shown in Figure 9.5 [8].

Figure 9.5 A typical 5G towers [8].

5G towers are telecommunications sites capable of transmitting 5G signals for wide-area coverage. 5G cell towers use a combination of low, mid, and high-frequency bands for various connectivity use cases. Towers themselves are not 5G; it is the equipment on the tower that makes it 5G. Figure 9.6 shows how 5G works [9].

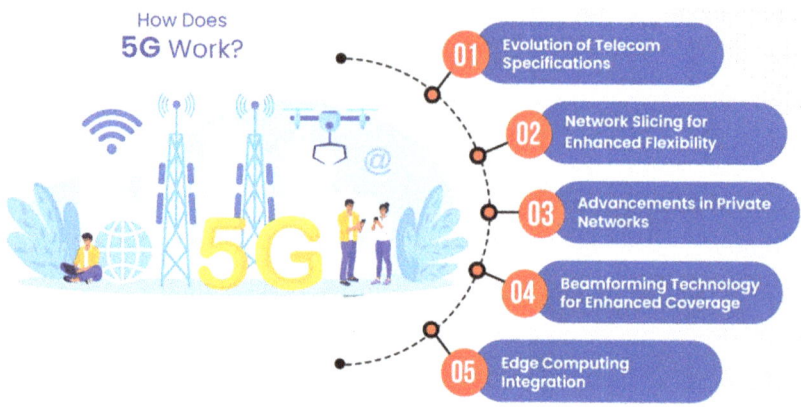

Figure 9.6 How 5G works [9].

In a 5G wireless network, every mobile phone will have an IPv6 address depending on the location and network being used. 5G utilizes the user-centric network concept World Wide Wireless Web (WWWW) instead of operator-centric as in 3G or service-centric as in 4G [10]. WWWW will be capable of supporting applications and services and interconnecting the whole world. 5G includes the latest technologies, such as cognitive radio, the Internet of things, nanotechnology, and cloud computing.

The key features of 5G include high throughput, improved spectrum efficiency, reduced latency, better mobility support, and high connection density. 5G technology has the following advanced features [11]:

- Architecture will be device-centric, distributed, programmable, and cloud-based

- High data rates

- One to 10 Gbps connections to endpoints

- One millisecond end-to-end round trip delay

- Low battery consumption

- Better connectivity irrespective of location

- Larger number of supporting devices

- Lower cost of infrastructure development

Some of these features are illustrated in Figure 9.7 [12]. The development of 5G will not be from scratch but will gradually build on 4G LTE. Major technologies enabling 5G include:

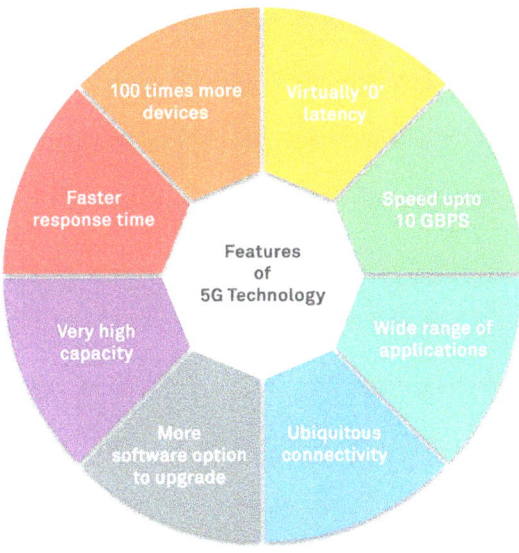

Figure 9.7 Some of the features of 5G [12].

- *D2D Communication:* Direct connectively is achieved through device-to-device (D2D) technology. 5G cellular network will implement D2D mm wave communication technology to provide high-speed data rate, improve coverage, and offer peer-to-peer services. Much research has been invested in characterizing D2D connections as part of LTE [13].

- *M2M Communication:* While D3D communication targets mobile radios, machine-to-machine (M2M) expands the scope and facilitates ubiquitous connectivity among mobile devices. It is estimated that there will be over 100 billion connected devices using M2M communications in the 5G backbone [14].

- *MIMO:* Multiple-input-multiple-output (MIMO) technology plays a crucial role in 4G and is expected to play an important function in 5G. Massive MIMO extracts the benefits of MIMO on a large scale by increasing the throughput and spectrum efficiency.

Other enabling technologies of 5G include mmWave communication, ultra-dense network (UDN), all-spectrum access (ASA), OFDM (orthogonal frequency division multiplexing), and the Internet of things. Industries that use 5G technology are shown in Figure 9.8 [5].

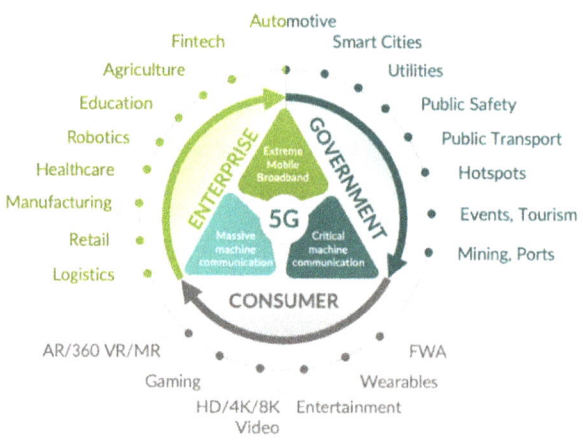

Figure 9.8 Industries that use 5G technology [5].

This section would be incomplete without mentioning the successors of 5G [15]:

- *6G Network:* Fifth-generation cellular technology is replaced by sixth-generation wireless or 6G. The bandwidth and latency of 6G networks will be significantly higher than those of 5G networks due to their ability to operate at higher frequencies. The main purpose of 6G internet is to provide communications with one-microsecond latency. 6G will employ satellites to connect the current 5G networks.

• *7G Network:* Globally, the 7G Network provides a faster means of communication. The advanced cellular technology that will be the successor for 5G and 6G. A 7G network is the quickest way to make a call, whether it is local or international. Voice over Internet Protocol (VoIP), or 7G, requires access to all local and international telecommunications. 7G will be able to satisfy the requirements of extremely high bandwidth, almost zero latency, and universal integration. Although 7G will not be generally available until 2030, a handful of countries are currently using it. These include Norway, Netherlands, South Korea, and Hungary. They are the nations in the world to provide the fastest Internet speeds.

9.3 5G NETWORK IN MEDIA AND ENTERTAINMENT

In today's fast-paced digital world, technology continues to evolve at an astonishing rate. With its promise of lightning-fast speeds, low latency, and enhanced connectivity, 5G is set to revolutionize the media and entertainment industries by facilitating new types of content creation and consumption, and by opening up existing markets to enterprising new players. As 5G technology takes root in North America, it presents transformative opportunities for media and broadcast companies, especially those in the middle-market sector. 5G will bring astonishing growth to the media and entertainment industries over the next few years. The enhanced, 5G networks have enabled users with faster streaming, new interactive experiences, including a revolution in mobile gaming, content creation, and accessibility by connecting all our internet connected devices more seamlessly. As shown in Figure 9.9, 5G is transforming entertainment landscape [16].

Figure 9.9 5G is transforming entertainment landscape [16].

Perhaps the clearest implementation of 5G in the immediate future will be the enhancement of streaming services. Today, we have become accustomed to streaming apps providing the majority of our favorite series. As the power of 5G connectivity becomes harnessed by the streaming world's leading apps, viewers can expect a revolution in how shows and movies can be watched, particularly on the go. 5G also brings greater network capacities that enable more ultra-high-definition (UHD) content for fully immersive streaming experiences. Through the use of integrated technology, we may soon see streaming services offer real-time entertainment experiences such as live or on-demand concerts, movie premieres, sporting events, and multiplayer video games [16]. As shown in Figure 9.10, 5G will change the business of media and entertainment [17].

5G will change the business of media and entertainment

Figure 9.10 5G will change the business of media and entertainment [17].

9.4 APPLICATIONS OF 5G NETWORK IN MEDIA AND ENTERTAINMENT

5G opens new pathways for the media and broadcast sector to push boundaries, enhance viewer experiences, and drive operational efficiency. By leveraging the capabilities of 5G, companies can enhance service delivery, streamline operations, optimize costs, and spur innovation, positioning themselves advantageously in an increasingly competitive landscape. Common application areas include the following [18-21]:

• *Live Productions:* Today's live productions can be complex, costly, and infrastructure-intensive endeavors. A vast array of resources and personnel are required to shoot a television show on location or broadcast a sporting event in progress, including production trucks, miles of cabling, specialty field gear and, of course, a full crew to configure it, operate it, maintain it, and then tear it all down again afterward. 5G network slicing could allow media and entertainment businesses to deliver live productions over the cellular communications network without compromising on the high standards that are required.

• *Remote Production:* Remote production involves filming a scene or a live event at one location and production and dissemination of that content happening at a different location. With remote production, filming is typically done with multiple remotely operated cameras that feed data to the cloud or a production facility where it is further processed and transmitted. 5G remote production offers the same reliability of cables with the convenience of being wireless. It also has the capability of transmitting data at a faster speed without compressing to maintain higher quality. Media and entertainment businesses could also use 5G network slicing to transform remote production workflows. In addition to ensuring cost-effective live production capabilities, this technology can also allow remotely located personnel to mix and edit content just as quickly and efficiently.

• *Content on Demand:* Content on demand is one of the most significant developments in media and entertainment over the last few years. As audiences demand superior quality, no buffering, and no outages, the adoption of 5G networks by content creators has become imperative. 5G offers the added advantage of seamless content streaming even in congested areas.

• *Power Streaming:* Our next generation will grow up in a world where they know nothing less than high speed, highly reliable connectivity. 5G will bring about new ways in which the younger generation consumes content thereby leading to new and innovative ways of content creation. The next generation of super creators will be able to take things to the next level with 5G.

• *Immersive Media:* Augmented reality (AR), virtual reality (VR) and the combination of the two called mixed reality (XR) are a new and much sought-after form of entertainment. Sports leagues and entertainment companies are exploring 5G network slicing's potential to bring the metaverse to life, beginning with fan experiences involving extended reality (XR) technologies such as AR and VR. Immersive experiences will rely on high-performing 5G network connections that can meet the low latency requirements associated with AR and VR environments.

• *Cloud-Based Gaming:* 5G has opened a world of possibilities for the rapidly growing gaming industry. 5G technology has the ability to create a platform-agnostic experience in gaming through cloud gaming. 5G is also the catalyst for a mobile gaming revolution, allowing gamers to play on-the-go with previously unseen connectivity and speed. The high speeds and low lag times of 5G are expected to provide a breakthrough for cloud-based gaming. 5G allows for cloud-based gaming, enabling users to stream games from remote servers with minimal latency. Cloud gaming services, like Steam, Xbox Live, and NVIDIA GeForce Now, can deliver a vast library of games to mobile devices. Video games require the transmission of large amounts of data and minimal latency in transmission for optimal playing experience. With 5G, complex processing can be done at a centralized server and transmitted seamlessly, directly to consumers. Perhaps more interestingly, video game developers may themselves decide to market directly to their customer base. Figure 9.11 shows an example of gaming [22].

Figure 9.11 An example of gaming [22].

• *Over-the-Top TV:* Another sector of the entertainment industry marked by a small number of dominant players is television distribution. With relatively few cable companies in a given area, consumers generally face little selection when choosing a television provider. Although over-the-top television ("OTT TV") has been gaining momentum in recent years, the attractiveness of these offerings has been limited by the fact that OTT TV service is currently still dependent on a hard-wired Internet connection. This has allowed cable companies to preserve their role across both the television and Internet service markets, and has constrained the value proposition of OTT TV.

9.5 BENEFITS

One of the key benefits of 5G network is its ability to handle high-bandwidth content, such as VR, AR and XR. 5G could help open up new business opportunities for the media and entertainment sector. 5G technology is set to revolutionize the way we consume media and content, with its faster speeds, lower latency, and enhanced connectivity. As the demand for video quality and the loading speed is rising, 5G technology has become mainstream. Other benefits of 5G for media & entertainment include the following [23]:

• *Personalized Experiences:* A key advantage that 5G supplies streaming services over traditional digital viewing comes in the form of personalization. For customers and businesses alike, personalized ads can help bring relevance and build better viewing experiences. 5G-powered networks can deliver personalized content and advertising, leading to increased viewer engagement and revenue opportunities. 5G can help make ads more intrinsic and personalized.

• *High-Quality Video Content:* One of the most significant advantages of 5G technology in the realm of media and content is its ability to support higher-quality video content. However, the bandwidth limitations of previous generations of wireless technology have often resulted in buffering issues and reduced video quality. 5G technology eliminates these concerns by providing faster speeds and greater capacity, allowing for uninterrupted streaming of 4K and even 8K resolution videos. 5G allows for higher-resolution streaming with minimal buffering and lag, offering a superior viewing experience. With the improvement in bandwidth and lower latency, media companies will be able to deliver more high-quality content to their audiences, which can lead to increased audience engagement.

• *Increased Speed:* 5G's lightning-fast speeds and ultra-low latency allow for rapid data transfer, empowering broadcast teams with real-time editing, streaming, and production tools. This leads to faster turnaround times and improved flexibility, especially critical for live events where agility and rapid response are essential.

• *Low Latency:* 5G delivers high-speed connectivity and ultra-low latency, making it ideal for live broadcasts and remote production. With 5G, the low latency and high bandwidth capabilities enable seamless VR and AR experiences, making them more accessible to a wider audience. From gaming to virtual tours and live events, 5G technology has the potential to transform the way we engage with digital content. With the improvement in bandwidth and lower latency, media companies will be able to deliver more high-quality content to their audiences, which can lead to increased audience engagement.

• *Accessibility:* With its improved transmission speeds and lower latency, the 5G network enables more widespread access to media content, particularly in rural and remote areas. This can lead to increased audience reach and opportunities for new business models.

• *Innovative Storytelling:* Interactive storytelling and personalized experiences are made possible by the low latency and high bandwidth capabilities of 5G. The advent of 5G technology in media and content will pave the way for innovative storytelling techniques. With faster speeds and reduced latency, content creators can explore new avenues for interactive storytelling.

• *Immersive Content:* 5G opens up new possibilities for immersive virtual reality (VR) and augmented reality (AR) experiences, making them more accessible to a wider audience. VR and AR technologies have gained traction in recent years, offering users a more interactive and immersive experience. 5G facilitates the creation and delivery of virtual reality (VR), augmented reality (AR), and other immersive experiences, such as interactive gaming and personalized content. Owing to the ability of 5G to deliver high-resolution graphics and faster loading times, the sky could well be the limit for the incorporation of TV series and movies into the world of virtual reality.

9.6 CHALLENGES

5G, while promising significant advancements in media and entertainment, faces several challenges. These include the need for infrastructure development, the cost of 5G devices and services, and the evolving nature of the technology. A challenge is to close the huge gaps between the promised performance and the current or imminent 5G network deployments. Live streaming and on-demand video face challenges such as buffering, lag, and poor quality, especially in high-traffic areas. Other challenges of 5G networks in M&E industry include the following [24]:

• *Limitations:* 5G is only available in a few urban locations around the world, and much of it is still a beta version. It will take longer for 5G to become mainstream since it necessitates large infrastructure modifications and relies on users purchasing new technology. Unfortunately, we still need to understand where we stand with this latest telecom discovery. Traditional content creation and production workflows often face limitations in terms of speed, efficiency, and collaboration.

• *Security:* The increased data transmission and interconnectedness of 5G raise concerns about data security and privacy. Robust cybersecurity measures are crucial to protect sensitive information and ensure user trust. Ensuring the security and privacy of data transmitted over 5G networks is crucial for protecting users from cyber threats. 5G itself is not a security risk. But the new technologies that will surround and be enabled by 5G could be. In fact, the future of mobile wireless cyber security will become nearly synonymous with media and entertainment cyber security. Of course, 5G will usher in a new world of devices that can be compromised, like headsets, glasses, holographic displays, and more. And these devices could be another new point of vulnerability and impact media and entertainment cybersecurity.

• *Device Compatibility:* With 5G's capacity to support large-scale IoT deployments, broadcasters can manage multiple connected devices—from cameras and sensors to editing stations and servers—more effectively. Not all devices are 5G-compatible, and the cost of 5G-capable devices can be a barrier for some consumers. The lack of standardized practices and interoperability between different 5G devices and platforms can hinder seamless content delivery.

• *Collaboration:* Collaboration between content creators, network providers, and technology companies is crucial for the successful integration of 5G into the entertainment industry. As a catalyst for collaboration, 5G powered technology will create a more efficient production process with the added benefit of reaching teammates in remote locations. 5G technology enables real-time collaboration, remote production, and high-resolution streaming, revolutionizing content creation workflows.

• *Infrastructure and Availability:* The widespread adoption of 5G is hindered by the need for further infrastructure development, especially in areas with limited access.

• *Cost and Affordability:* The cost of 5G-enabled devices and subscription plans remains relatively high, potentially limiting access for some users.

9.7 CONCLUSION

The 5G revolution is taking the world by storm. From streaming high-quality videos to immersive virtual reality experiences, 5G technology has the potential to reshape the entertainment industry as we know it. In the era of digital transformation, the media and entertainment industry is experiencing a seismic shift propelled by the proliferation of 5G technology. The global deployment of 5G technologies is a certainty. As we have seen with every wireless generation shift before, this will drive the proliferation of richer entertainment, media, and advertising experiences.

Even though 5G networks are not yet widely available, most media and marketing professionals believe they will change the way entertainment, sports, and news are produced, disseminated, and consumed in the future. 5G technology is poised to revolutionize the broadcasting media industry in several ways. With its improved bandwidth and lower latency, it allows for faster and more reliable streaming of media content. As the demand for video quality and the loading speed is rising, 5G technology will become mainstream. 5G is changing the business of broadcasting entertainment and transforming the audience experience. With the dawn of 5G, a new vision of the future of media and entertainment will be defined. To stay ahead in this rapidly evolving landscape, it is essential for professionals in the media and content industry to stay informed and adapt to changes. More information on the implementation of 5G networks in the M&E industry is available from the books in [25-29].

REFERENCES

[1] "The 5G revolution: Taking the entertainment industry by storm," March 2023,

https://www.linkedin.com/pulse/5g-revolution-taking-entertainment-industry-storm-teamleasedigital/

[2] M. Katibeh, "Lights, camera, 5G: Transforming the entertainment industry with 5G," November 2019,

https://www.forbes.com/councils/forbestechcouncil/2019/11/27/lights-camera-5g-transforming-the-entertainment-industry-with-5g/

[3] "5G Technology: Mastering the magic triangle,"

https://www.reply.com/fr/telco-and-media/5g-mastering-the-magic-triangle

[4] M. N. O. Sadiku, S. A. Ajayi, and J. O. Sadiku, "5G network in media and entertainment," *International Journal of Scientific and Academic Research*, vol. 5, no. 5, August 2025, pp. 15-27.

[5] "[Burning issue] 5G technology,"

https://www.civilsdaily.com/burning-issue-5g-technology-2/

[6] "5G technology and networks (speed, use cases, rollout)," September 2024,

https://www.thalesgroup.com/en/markets/digital-identity-and-security/mobile/inspired/5G#:~:text=5G%20connectivity%20promises%20to%20break,in%20delivery%2C%20and%20complete%20interoperability.

[7] R. S. Sapakal and S. S. Kadam, "5G mobile technology," *International Journal of Advanced Research in Computer Engineering & Technology*, vol. 2, no. 2, February 2013, pp. 568-571.

[8] K. Kimachia, "Top 8 5G issues and disadvantages to know

before switching," June 2023,

https://www.enterprisenetworkingplanet.com/management/top-issues-facing-5g-networks/

[9] "5G use cases paving the way for technological advancements,"

https://www.veritis.com/blog/5g-use-cases-paving-way-for-technological-advancements/

[10] "How 5G technology works,"

https://www.rfpage.com/how-5g-technology-works/

[11] D. H. Latha et al., "A study on 5th generation mobile technology – Future network service," *International Journal of Computer Science and Information Technologies*, vol. 5, no. 6, 2014, pp. 8309-8313.

[12] "Guest blog: Business @ speed of thought: The power of 5G, Edge, and IoT," December 2020,

https://www.techuk.org/resource/guest-blog-business-speed-of-thought-the-power-of-5g-edge-and-iot.html

[13] S. Andreev, "Delivering uniform connectively and service experience to converged 5G wireless networks," *Proceedings of the IEEE World Forum on Internet of Things*, 2014, pp. 323-324.

[14] M. H. Alsharif et al., "How to make key wireless technologies environmental friendly: a review," *Transactions of Emerging Telecommunications Technologies*, vol. 29, 2018.

[15] A. Kayyali, "Countries using 7G network technology today," October 2022,

https://insidetelecom.com/countries-using-7g-network-technology-today/

[16] "The 5G revolution: Taking the entertainment industry by storm,"

https://www.linkedin.com/pulse/5g-revolution-taking-entertainment-industry-storm-teamleasedigital/

[17] "5G will change the business of media and entertainment," July 2019,

https://www.faistgroup.com/news/5g-will-change-the-business-of-media-and-entertainment/

[18] D. Solvid, "Why the 5G era will revolutionize television and entertainment as we know it," March 2024,

https://datafloq.com/read/5g-revolutionize-television-entertainment/

[19] "5G media and entertainment,"

https://www.jio.com/business/5g/5g-industry/5g-media-and-entertainment/

[20] R. de Fremery, "How 5G network slicing could benefit the media and entertainment industry," March 2024,

https://www.verizon.com/business/resources/articles/s/how-5g-network-slicing-benefits-media-and-entertainment-industry/

[21] A. Miller, J. L. Richter, and K. Schneider, "5G and the future of entertainment," January 2019,

https://www.akingump.com/en/insights/blogs/ag-deal-diary/5g-and-the-future-of-entertainment

[22] "The impact of 5G on media technology," November 2023,

https://mediatech.edu/the-impact-of-5g-on-media-technology/

[23] "The impact of 5G technology on media and content," September 2023,

https://www.yellowbrick.co/blog/entertainment/the-impact-of-5g-technology-on-media-and-content

[24] "How 5G revolutionized digital content delivery in the media and entertainment industry?" May 2024,

https://p99soft.com/unleashing-the-power-of-5g/

[25] W. Jiang and B. Han, *Cellular Communication Networks and*

Standards: The Evolution from 1G to 6G. Springer, 2024.

[26] W. Chen et al., *Fundamentals of 5G Communications: Connectivity for Enhanced Mobile Broadband and Beyond*. McGraw Hill LLC, 2021.

[27] J. Penttinen, *5G Simplified: ABCs of Advanced Mobile Communications*. Kindle Edition, 2019.

[28] M. A. Imran, Q. H. Abbasi, and Y. A. Sambo, *Enabling 5G Communication Systems to Support Vertical Industries*. Wiley, 2019.

[29] A. F. Molisch, *Wireless Communications: From Fundamentals to Beyond 5G*. Wiley-IEEE Press; 3rd edition, 2022.

CHAPTER 10
BIOMETRICS IN
MEDIA AND ENTERTAINMENT

"No two snowflakes are exactly alike. No two people's fingerprints are exactly the same. And therein lies our greatest superpower. When we discover our own unique gift and purpose, connected to the wisdom of Divinity itself, there is no competition."

— Anonymous

10.1 INTRODUCTION

Hollywood produces great entertainment. The United States media and entertainment (M&E) industry is a $703 billion market, comprised of businesses that produce and distribute motion pictures, television programs and commercials, streaming content, music and audio recordings, broadcast, radio, book publishing, video games and supplementary services and products. The M&E industry can be partitioned into four main verticals: film, music, book publishing and video games, as illustrated in Figure 10.1 [1]. The M&E industry is large and varied, constantly under pressure to innovate and explore emerging technologies for the potential impact on development.

MEDIA & ENTERTAINMENT

■ Film ■ TV ■ Video Games ■ Music ■ Publishing

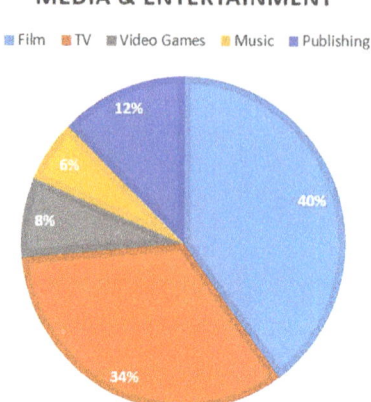

Figure 10.1 The media and entertainment industry [1].

Biometrics refer to the unique physical characteristics of a person, which could include fingerprints or facial recognition information. They offer solutions for identity verification, access control, and even personalization of content. For example, Apple's current range of devices use biometric authentication for easier device access.

Biometric technology involves the use of physiological or behavioral characteristics, such as fingerprints, facial recognition, iris scans, voice recognition, or DNA, to identify individuals. Biometrics are playing a growing role not only in the real-time policing and securing of increasingly crowded and varied venues worldwide, but also in ensuring a smooth, enjoyable experience for the citizens who visit them.

Biometrics, like fingerprints, facial recognition, and retinal scans, are increasingly used in the media and entertainment industry for a variety of purposes, including enhancing security, streamlining user experiences, and personalizing content. With biometric technologies, media organizations can enhance authentication, verification, and identification processes, thereby ensuring the integrity and reliability of information disseminated through digital platforms [2].

This chapter examines various uses of biometrics in media and entertainment. It begins with explaining what biometrics are and their various types. It describes biometrics in the media and entertainment industry and provides some applications. It highlights the benefits and challenges of biometrics in media and entertainment. The last section concludes with comments.

10.2 WHAT ARE BIOMETRICS?

Any banking customer has used a password or a PIN code at least once. However, these traditional methods of verification are steadily giving way to the next generation of authorization tools. Passwords, codes, PINs, and safety questions have shown to be less dependable when used against modern cybersecurity threats. The financial sector is shifting towards safer, more customer-friendly verification. Biometric authentication has arisen as an answer to the outdated and more easily compromised traditional techniques.

Biometrics is the utilization of unique biological traits for identification. It is a technology powered method of personal identification that leverages unique biological patterns on and in human body. It is based on one-of-a-kind biological characteristics of a client, which include fingerprints, facial traits, and more. It is a fast-developing field that utilizes users' unique biological characteristics, like fingerprints, facial features, iris patterns, or even voice, to identify and verify the users. This technology is poised to become just as common in the world of financial transactions, where convenience is key and security is paramount. It offers a significant leap forward compared to traditional passwords and PINs. It promises a future of banking that is not only exceptionally secure but also remarkably convenient and personalized. Figure 10.2 shows a representation of biometrics [3].

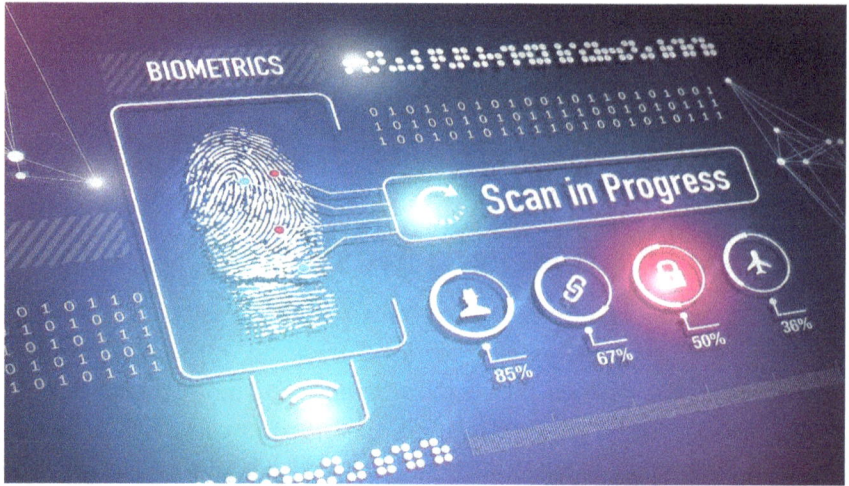

Figure 10.2 A presentation of biometrics [3].

Biometric payments date to ancient civilizations, in which physical traits such as handprints and facial features were used for identification. Modern biometrics emerged in the 1800s and biometric payment systems began to gain traction in the early 2000s, when Pay By Touch introduced one of the first fingerprint-based payment systems. By the 2020s, biometric technology has become widespread and is integrated into smartphones for a variety of applications including payment authentication. Today, biometric payments are more popular and widely adopted than ever.

Biometric authentication employs cutting-edge technology to capture and analyze various biological attributes. Two main hardware setups allow biometric payments to work. The first uses the built-in hardware on a customer's smartphone or smart device, such as a fingerprint scanner or facial recognition, to authenticate their identity. The second scenario uses dedicated payment system hardware to verify a person using biometrics. When a user attempts to access a financial service, such as logging into an online banking account or making a transaction, the system prompts them to provide a biometric sample. This sample is compared against the stored biometric template for that individual. Access is granted if there is a match; if not, the system denies access.

10.3 TYPES OF BIOMETRICS

Biometrics in financial digital services concerns the protection of users' financial and personal data and the conduct of financial transactions. The different types of biometric payments include [4]:

• *Fingerprint Recognition:* A fingerprint biometric is a representation of multiple points on the fingerprint, and the relative positions of those points. Fingerprint recognition is the most common form of biometric payment. It involves scanning and matching the unique patterns on a person's fingertip or fingertips to authenticate their identity and authorize a transaction. Fingerprint biometrics in finance offer several benefits to financial institutions and their customers. Figure 10.3 shows fingerprint biometrics [5].

Figure 10.3 Fingerprint biometrics [5].

• *Facial Recognition:* This technology works similarly to how our eyes and brains identify people. First popularized by Apple's Face ID, this method is quickly catching up to fingerprint recognition in popularity. It works by using infrared light to scan a person's face and pinpoint thousands of dots that make up their unique facial structure. The traits are transformed into a template for subsequent authorization. If the features are nearly identical, the admission is authorized. With face recognition technology, computer vision is used to create a biometric template of a user's face, measuring unvarying characteristics such as the distance between the eyes and the length of the nose. Figure 10.4 shows facial recognition [6].

Figure 10.4 Facial recognition biometrics [6].

• *Retina Recognition:* This is also known as eye scanning. Its essence is to check people based on the unique patterns found on their irises. By capturing the intricate patterns within the iris or retina, this method offers a high level of accuracy in authenticating users, and has long been trusted in high-security environments. A special camera captures the iris in high definition, and the resulting image is matched up with the pre-existing framework. If they are mostly identical, the client is allowed onto the application. Airports originally used iris scanning for security screening. However, it has now become part of banking security.

• *Voice Recognition:* This method is based on the vocal traits of users. The pitch of voice modulation, as well as speaking habits, help create a voiceprint for further verification. The method analyzes the nuances in speech patterns and voice characteristics, then compares this voiceprint to registered samples to certify a match.

• *Behavioral Recognition:* A client's behavior patterns have unique dynamics online, including typing rhythm, mouse/ touchscreen use, speech, or walking. Unlike the other biometric authentication examples, this one takes into consideration the interaction with versatile systems and devices. A behavioral profile is established and then utilized for authorization. Behavioral recognition is non-disruptive and highly secure because of its resistance to forgery.

• *Vein Patterns:* Using near-infrared light and often centering on the palm or finger, this technology analyzes the pattern of visible blood vessels unique to each person.

• *Signature Recognition:* This somewhat less common process scans and digitizes a person's signature, then puts it through a shape-identifying algorithm to verify their identity.

• *Palm Recognition:* Similar to fingerprint scanning, this verification type relies on capturing the individual traits of the client's palm. It embraces patterns, ridges, loops, and other modalities. They are very precise and difficult to reproduce. Rich in detail and complex, these contribute to the successful identification.

Figure 10.5 shows some of these types of biometric authentication [7].

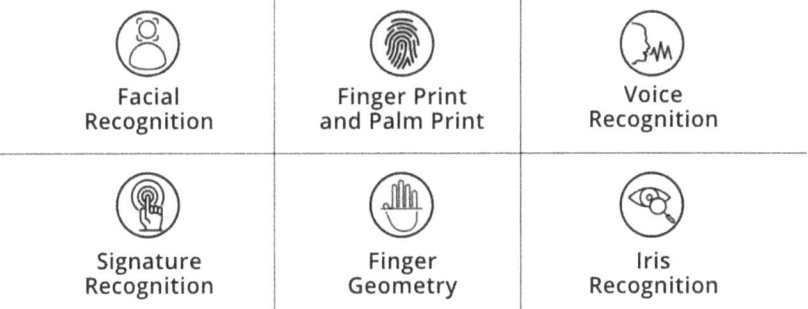

Figure 10.5 Types of biometric authentication [7].

10.4 BIOMETRICS IN MEDIA AND ENTERTAINMENT

Biometrics encompass a variety of different technologies that use probabilistic matching to recognize a person based on their biometric characteristics. Biometric characteristics can be physiological features (for example, a person's fingerprint, iris, face or hand geometry), or behavioral attributes (such as a person's gait, signature, or keystroke pattern). The use of biometric technologies and systems is expanding significantly within the public and private sectors. Biometric technologies, such as facial recognition, voice, fingerprint or iris scanning technologies, are becoming cheaper, more advanced, and more accurate. As a result, they are becoming more integrated into people's daily lives, and in their interactions with government. Behavioral biometrics are increasingly being used for passive authentication, often as an additional layer of security.

10.5 APPLICATIONS OF BIOMETRICS IN MEDIA AND ENTERTAINMENT

Biometric technology has numerous applications in the entertainment industry, ranging from enhancing audience engagement to improving security and personalization. Common applications of biometric technology in media and entertainment include the following:

• *Live Events:* Biometrics are increasingly being adopted for use at sports and other live events. The technology is being used to enhance ticketing, credentialing, and sales of concessions, merchandise, and alcohol. Go-Ahead Entry, which links facial recognition with ticket accounts to make the process touchless, quick and secure, is just one example of how digital identity verification and blockchain-based ticketing are helping stadium operators enhance the fan experience. An example of a live event is shown in Figure 10.6 [8].

Figure 10.6 A live event [8].

• *Personalization:* Biometric data can be used to tailor content recommendations, adjust settings, and even personalize the user experience in virtual environments. Biometric facial recognition technology is being used in the entertainment industry to personalize the user experience. For example, facial recognition technology can be used to identify a person and provide personalized recommendations for movies or music based on their interests and preferences. Personalizing the user experience using biometric technology involves using an individual's unique biometric data to tailor the content, services, or products they receive. As for personalized advertising, biometric data can also be used to personalize advertising based on an individual's interests and preferences. Figure 10.7 shows an example of personalization [8].

Figure 10.7 An example of personalization [8].

• *Biometric Authentication:* Social media apps may contain a lot of personal and sensitive data, which, if compromised, can have many negative impacts on a user. Securing this information is as important as securing an email account or an ecommerce account. Before the rise of biometric authentication, social media apps used password/PIN based authentication. Entering passwords on touch screen devices is hardly a user friendly experience, if users can recollect today's complex passwords at all. Biometric authentication on mobile devices has solved this problem and has improved the authentication process dramatically.

10.6 BENEFITS

Countries around the world are using biometrics to streamline entertainment. For example, London is using biometrics to streamline ticketing during sporting events. Many biometric parameters of a person may be used by modern technology for identifying people, but they vary in cost, speed, and accuracy of usage. Another benefit is that biometric characteristics cannot be as easily shared, lost, or duplicated as passwords or tokens. Other benefits of biometrics in media and entertainment include the following [10,11]:

• *Easy to Use:* Biometric technology is straightforward to use. While they are primarily found in high-security spots, like airports, hospitals, and similar, everyday items like smartphones, tablets, and laptops utilize biometrics. Both Android and iOS devices use different forms of biometric technology, such as fingerprint and facial scanning, which means users no longer have to type out a passcode to access their phones. Some financial and messaging apps, too, use biometric technology to allow users to gain access instead of typing out their passwords. This makes the user experience surrounding biometric technology so much more appealing.

• *Easy to Integrate:* Many software applications use biometrics, and because it is available for use across multiple platforms, it is relatively easy to secure your accounts in just one tap. Those with smart homes will also appreciate how easy it is to integrate biometrics into several IoT devices at home.

• *Difficult to Fake:* Biometric technology is relatively hard to fake and spoof. While not impossible, facial patterns, irises, and fingerprints are difficult to replicate and could take more effort than necessary. While some phones can be unlocked with photos, consumer technology companies can prevent this by improving their technology in general. For example, most smartphones use 2D facial recognition scanning technology. Still, in the future, more smartphones might adopt 3D facial recognition instead to make it even harder for hackers to spoof things.

• *High-security Assurance:* Because biometrics rely on fingerprints, irises, and other unique human features; they can be a better option than passwords for protecting accounts. When paired with other forms of multi-factor authentication (MFA), you can also add another layer of security that is more difficult for others to hack. Because biometric authentication generally requires a living, breathing human to be present, it can be pretty tricky for AI or other forms of technology to spoof.

• *Security:* Biometrics help verify user identities, mitigating risks like impersonation and identity theft. This can be crucial for securing access to content, platforms, and events. Biometrics can also be used to enhance safety measures, such as monitoring crowd density or identifying individuals on watchlists.

• *Behavior:* Emotions drive behavior, despite what we think. Appetite for good content is fierce. Viewer attention spans are short and getting shorter. Audiences are consuming media across multiple channels. As media consumption increases, the brands that survive will be the ones that are able to forge stronger emotional connections.

• *Personalized Experiences:* One of the most powerful applications of facial recognition in media is its ability to deliver personalized experiences and targeted marketing campaigns. This allows content distributors to create more engaging and relevant experiences for their audiences.

10.7 CHALLENGES

Facial recognition is surrounded by tons of baggage. The use of facial recognition in the real world is fraught with concerns about misuse, particularly when in the hands of law enforcement. The use of biometric technology raises several legal issues that need to be carefully considered and addressed to ensure that individuals' rights are protected. The potential negative impacts of biometrics include privacy, security, as well as ethical norms. Cultural or religious factors may also limit a group or individual's ability to participate or enroll in a biometric system. Another limitation of biometric systems is that unlike passwords or ID tokens, biometric characteristics cannot be reissued or cancelled. Other challenges faced by biometrics in media and entertainment include the following [11,12]:

• *Costs:* To maintain and sustain a strong security profile, companies will have to spend significant money to ensure software and hardware are up to date. Beyond companies, biometric security can also be expensive for personal use. Prices for biometric access control systems like electronic doors and installation could cost upwards of 2,500 US dollars.

• *Ethical Concern:* Ensuring ethical use and fairness of

biometrics necessitates mandatory periodic assessments of biometric algorithms for bias and discrimination, particularly in high-stake scenarios such as law enforcement and employment.

• *Governance:* This is another important element to consider when adopting and using biometrics; the oversight and accountability of systems is critical to ensuring they are used appropriately. Organizations using biometric systems should have transparent complaints and enquiry systems in place, and identify the appropriate internal and external avenues for redress, in case of misuse of biometric information or faults in the biometric system.

• *Legal Challenges:* As biometric technology is increasingly being used in various industries, including healthcare, banking, security, and law enforcement, there are several legal issues that arise in the collection, storage, and use of biometric data. With this expanding market for biometrics has come an abundance of legal questions, as state laws are in flux. Some states have laws in place, while others are in the process of implementing laws. The lack of strict legislation and prominent use of biometrics in popular interfaces has led to several lawsuits involving user privacy. Statutes tend to prevent use of personal biometric data without consent.

• *Trust:* The issue of trust in media has generated a substantial body of research that has investigated the causes and effects of trust in media. The contemporary media landscape is grappling with a severe crisis characterized by the proliferation of misinformation, a decline in public trust, and the rampant spread of fake news, largely fueled by social media platforms. Biometric technology offers unique advantages in restoring trust in media. Biometrics, with its capabilities in identity verification, content authentication, mitigation of bots and Sybil attacks, and creation of personalized user experiences, offers unique advantages to restore trust, combat misinformation, and establish a secure online media ecosystem. The film industry in general is not recognized for its commitment to truth, and Hollywood's depiction of biometric technology is no exception.

• *Privacy:* The main concern of biometric information dissemination focuses on the protection of personal data. The abuse, tampering and leakage of personal and corporate data have triggered public concern about technical risks. Biometric data is highly personal and sensitive information, and therefore, the collection, storage, and use of such data may violate an individual's right to privacy. Many countries have enacted laws that regulate the use of biometric data and require companies to obtain individuals' consent before collecting their biometric information.

• *Data Security:* Protecting the security of biometric information is essential given its inherent and delicate nature. Biometric systems remain vulnerable at the perception, network, and application layers, posing a significant threat to the security of the Internet of things (IoT) and social networks. Biometric data can be hacked or stolen, just like any other personal data. Therefore, companies that collect and store biometric data need to take appropriate measures to secure such data from unauthorized access, disclosure, or misuse.

• *Data Quality:* This ensures that the personal information organizations hold is accurate, complete, and up to date. Data quality is particularly important at the enrollment stage, as the quality of a biometric sample will impact on the accuracy and effectiveness of the biometric system. For example, a low-quality biometric sample at the time of enrollment can increase the risk of false acceptance and false rejection in future presentations for authentication or identification. There are some factors that may affect the quality of a biometric sample, including low quality sensors or environmental conditions.

• *Perceived Risks:* Biometric technology pose risks as well as opportunities. Although biometrics offers some advantages for identity management, it is not a bullet-proof solution for fraud or identity theft. In the field of communication, perceived risks are included in our framework as an individual's subjective evaluation of potential negative outcomes or uncertainties associated with biometric technology services. Another privacy risk is the covert or passive collection of individuals' biometric information without their consent, participation, or knowledge.

10.8 CONCLUSION

Biometric identification is a signal for advancements we have yet to reach, and rather than think about the issues they could bring when deployed, we only focus on the optimistic possibilities. While biometric systems are becoming more effective as technology advances, they are not a foolproof method of authentication or identification.

Advancements in biometrics will likely open up even more opportunities for innovation in the entertainment industry. User adoption of biometrics is an increasing trend. More information on biometrics in media and entertainment can be found in the books in [13-16].

REFERENCES

[1] "Media and entertainment industry overview,"

https://investmentbank.com/media-and-entertainment-industry-overview/

[2] M. N. O. Sadiku, P. A. Adekunte, and J. O. Sadiku, "Biometrics in media and entertainment," *International Journal of Trend in Scientific Research and Development*, vol. 9, no. 3, May-June 2025, pp. 885-892.

[3] D. Orme, "The death of the PIN,"

https://internationaldirector.com/technology/the-death-of-the-pin/

[4] "Biometric payments: What are they and how are they shaping the future of commerce?" March 2024,

https://www.payset.io/post/biometric-payments-how-are-they-shaping-the-future-of-commerce

[5] "Fingerprint biometrics in finance: Balancing security and convenience in a digital world,"

https://theenterpriseworld.com/how-fingerprint-biometrics-in-finance-work/

[6] "Face recognition,"

https://www.nec.com/en/global/solutions/biometrics/face/index.html

[7] "How biometrics in banking is redefining security and user experience?" April 2025

https://www.appventurez.com/biometrics-in-banking

[8] "Global live events industry focuses on biometrics in 2025," January 2025,

https://www.pymnts.com/news/biometrics/2025/global-live-events-industry-focuses-biometrics/

[9] "The pros and cons of biometrics," June 2025,

https://ceoworld.biz/2022/05/09/the-pros-and-cons-of-biometrics/

[10] S. Shilina, "Biometrics: A beacon of trust in the digital media crisis," April 2024,

https://medium.com/@sshshln/biometrics-a-beacon-of-trust-in-the-digital-media-crisis-10f13ebe81d5

[11] F. Permata, "Biometric technology in the entertainment industry," March 2023,

https://medium.com/@fapermata/biometric-technology-in-the-entertainment-industry-345b2777dd68

[12] "Biometrics and privacy – Issues and challenges,"

https://ovic.vic.gov.au/privacy/resources-for-organisations/biometrics-and-privacy-issues-and-challenges/

[13] W. Rodgers, *Biometric and Auditing Issues Addressed in a Throughput Model*. Information Age Publishing, 2011.

[14] K. Gates, *Our Biometric Future: Facial Recognition Technology and the Culture of Surveillance*. NYU Press, 2011.

[15] Information Resources Management Association (ed.), *Biometrics: Concepts, Methodologies, Tools*, and Applications. IGI Global, 2016.

[16] M. Gofman and S. Mitra (eds.), *Biometrics in a Data Driven World: Trends, Technologies, and Challenges*. Boca Raton, FL: CRC Press, 2016.

INDEX

www.ingramcontent.com/pod-product-compliance
Lightning Source LLC
Chambersburg PA
CBHW051145120626
46547CB00012B/945